Do They Keep Kosher on Mars?

Do They Keep Kosher on Mars?

And Other Pressing Questions of Jewish Life

SOL the ANSWER MAN

Illustrated by Scott Matern

COLLIER BOOKS

MACMILLAN PUBLISHING COMPANY   NEW YORK

COLLIER MACMILLAN CANADA   TORONTO

MAXWELL MACMILLAN INTERNATIONAL

NEW YORK   OXFORD   SINGAPORE   SYDNEY

Collier Books
Macmillan Publishing Company
866 Third Avenue, New York, NY 10022

Collier Macmillan Canada, Inc.
1200 Eglinton Avenue East, Suite 200
Don Mills, Ontario M3C 3N1

Library of Congress Cataloging-in-Publication Data
Besser, James David.
Do they keep kosher on Mars? / James David Besser.
p.   cm.
ISBN 0-02-028155-2
1. Jews—Miscellanea. 2. Judaism—Miscellanea. 3. Jewish wit and
humor.   I. Title.
DS102.95.B47   1990   90-42405 CIP
001.9   909'.04924'00207—dc20

Macmillan books are available at special discounts for bulk purchases for sales
promotions, premiums, fund-raising, or educational use. For details, contact:

Special Sales Director
Macmillan Publishing Company
866 Third Avenue
New York, NY 10022

First Collier Books Edition 1990
10 9 8 7 6 5 4 3 2 1
Printed in the United States of America

To Karen, who has put up with a
know-it-all for two decades,
and to Nina, who is just
learning how.

Contents

T W O

Back Roads and Side Trips Through Jewish History

T H R E E

A Peculiar People: Strange Jewish Facts, Strange Jews

FOUR

The Unbearable Weirdness of Being: Strange Facts About Life at the End of the Twentieth Century

FIVE

Yiddish, English, and Other Exotic Languages

SIX

Holidays—Jewish and Otherwise

SEVEN

Strange Science and Technology:
Questions Too Hot for Mr. Wizard

Contents

EIGHT

Who Is a Jew, and Where the Heck Is He or She? A Mishmash of Figures About Jews

NINE

The Jewish Family and the Family of Jews: Jewish Family Life, Jewish Denominational Life

Contents

T E N
"I Fought the Law and the Law Won": A Highly Cursory Cruise Through Jewish Law

ELEVEN

Tradi-Tion, Tradition, Tra-Di-Tion:
A Potpourri of Jewish Traditions and Customs

TWELVE

Adventures and Mis-Adventures in Jewish Eating

Introduction

Q *Sol, just who the heck are you to distill thousands of years of Jewish tradition, not to mention most of Western civilization, into smart-aleck answers?*

A Sol is just a simple Answer Man, doing a dirty job that needs to be done.

Answer Men are ordinary folk with a lot of curiosity and the chutzpah to pursue questions that would embarrass mere mortals.

Answer Men are not authorities on anything, but semiauthorities on everything, with Rolodexes filled with the names and numbers of real experts.

Please be assured that Sol is an expert in no area at all. He is what some people might call a "Renaissance man," if they were given to absurd exaggeration.

Sol is not a rabbi, a Talmudic scholar, or an expert in

Jewish law. Some rabbis spend entire lifetimes disputing minor points of *Halachah;* as you point out, Sol's quick answers are not intended to put these guys out of business.

One would be ill-advised to make any major life decisions on the basis of Sol's pronouncements. That's what doctors, lawyers, and rabbis get paid for.

Sol believes that all of the different expressions of Judaism have something to offer in a world where Donald Trump and McDonald's sometime seem like the pinnacles of Western culture.

Sol also believes there is humor in every corner of Jewish life, and that strong and self-confident people don't mind poking a little fun at themselves.

Sol admires the Jewish quest for knowledge, but suspects that all too often it leads to intellectual hothouses for the few, and blissful ignorance for the many.

Sol's answers are for the curious masses, not yeshiva students. If you qualify, please read on.

Judaism Confronts the Space Age, the Stone Age, and the New Age

Q *Sol, Orthodox Jews believe the story of Genesis in a literal sense—that is, that the world is only a bit less than 6,000 years old. What do they say about dinosaurs and fossils?*

A Sol has generally maintained that there's nothing as easy as ridiculing religious orthodoxy—until some clown of a scientist sheepishly reveals that, "Hey, this whole theory was a mistake, sorry folks . . ."

To get specific: the strictly Orthodox view held by groups like the Lubavitcher Chasidim is that the world is almost 6,000 years old, which means that someone in the Smithsonian has miscalculated the age of their prize specimens by a few million years.

An Orthodox rabbi Sol consulted stoutly maintained that evidence for the age of dinosaur bones is far more tenuous than the scientist would have us believe. He pointed out that the scientific data is based on little bits and pieces of the beasts' bones—and a lot of extrapolation.

Scientists counter with arguments about carbon dating and other high-tech razzmatazz. The Orthodox thinkers respond by asking this question: who ever said earth's conditions were the same *before* the Flood as they are today? Could not carbon have had different molecular qualities? Isn't the carbon-dating process based on today's environment, not the world that existed before the Flood? After all, the Flood was accompanied by all kinds of environmental upheavals besides rain.

The bottom line, at least as far as the strictly Orthodox viewpoint goes, is that the earth was created in a developed state almost 6,000 years ago. As to the mystery of fossils and relics—well, they're just mysteries, among the many God has given us to ponder.

Remember, bubbe, this is not the view of Jews everywhere. Many Orthodox and Conservative Jews continue looking for ways to reconcile the story of creation with the modern scientific viewpoint, a quest that tends to make the eyeballs spin wildly in their sockets.

And most Reform Jews agree with the rest of the world that dinosaurs lived millions of years ago, specifically to give modern children something to babble about.

Q *Lately we've been hearing a lot about scientists patenting new forms of life. Maybe some laboratory will even clone a decent Answer Man. How many new species are there as a result of this technology? What does Jewish tradition have to say about this?*

A Not much, to put your last question first, and to ignore the ineffectual barb. Orthodox Judaism takes a dim view of monkeying with God's prerogative of creation—though some Jewish thinkers, recognizing the potential health benefits of genetic research, are working hard to reconcile medical ethics with theology.

Sol has not been able to locate a definitive count of new life forms generated in the laboratory. Remember, these aren't dogs or turtles we're talking about, but slimy things like bacteria and the like. There could be a million variations of a single microbe without you or Sol noticing a whit of difference.

But one measure may be the number of life forms patented. To date, some 400 organisms have received the blessing of the U.S. Patent Office. Sol wonders if the golem of MIT may be next.

***

Q *What does the Torah have to say about extra-terrestrial life? If we do contact life forms on other planets, does Jewish law give some hints about how we should approach them?*

A Very carefully, to answer the last part of your question first. Jewish law is not big on reckless behavior.

Although Jewish law does not speak directly to the question of extra-terrestrial life, scholars have interpolated the law to cover the subject. Basically, they have considered two aspects of the extra-terrestrial problem—whether or not advanced life is even possible in the cosmos, and how the discovery of Little Green Men from Alpha Centauri might affect the warp and woof of Judaism.

Not surprisingly, opinion seems to be divided along traditional theological lines. According to the Orthodox view, the Jewish faith precludes the possibility of superior life forms on other planets. Intelligent life requires the guidance of Torah— and the Torah was given exclusively to earthlings, not to inhabitants of far-flung planets.

Also, a belief in ETs implies the validity of evolution, a concept that wins no points with Orthodox thinkers. The Torah doesn't say anything about a Garden of Eden on Pluto.

According to a more modern interpretation, Jewish tradi-

tion doesn't emphasize the uniqueness of man, thus opening the door to the possibility of advanced life in the cosmos. According to Rabbi Norman Lamm, who has written a detailed treatise on the subject, Jewish tradition teaches that man is a mere "drop in the bucket" in the face of the awesome expanse of the universe.

In other words, so what if there are aliens with IQs measured in the millions, and no-wax floors that really stay clean? Big deal.

Rabbi Lamm emphasizes the notion that Judaism is uniquely equipped to withstand the culture shock of encounters with extra-terrestrial life. In fact, he writes, the discovery of advanced life "will deepen and broaden our appreciation of the mysteries of the Creator and His creations."

※

Q *Dear Sol: What do Jewish thinkers have to say about the idea of cryobiology—the idea that if I get some incurable disease, I can be flash-frozen, and then thawed when some genius comes up with a cure?*

A Sorry to throw cold water on your idea, but Jewish thinkers have given the idea of medical cryobiology a somewhat chilly reception, although the matter is far from settled.

As you might expect, the concept of freezing people introduces a number of ethical and moral problems. For instance, in freezing a person before death, are we hastening his death, something that would clearly be forbidden? Or are we unnaturally delaying the inevitable, another no-no in Jewish law?

Look at it another way: freezing the body and sticking it in a deep freeze could also be viewed as preventing a timely burial, something that is important in Jewish law.

And the idea that you might be hanging around for the next forty years in cold storage could wreak havoc on your family. Would your wife be a widow, or merely a woman whose husband was giving her the cold shoulder? Do your kids inherit your vast wealth, or does it hang around until you are thawed? You can see how it gets sticky.

On the other hand, terminally ill patients with no hope of survival might have a chance of restoration and cure at some later date through the freezing process. Judaism places a big emphasis on the necessity of saving lives, even when that requires bending Jewish law.

But is engaging in an experimental procedure of this sort, with no solid indication that it will actually work, a matter of protecting life, or just delaying burial?

This should give you a little flavor of the halachic debate that has taken place around the issue of cryobiology. Should *you* try it? Sol suggests intensive counseling with your rabbi, your doctor, and the guy who wants to turn you into an ice cube.

※

Q *What does Jewish law say about cosmetic surgery, like face-lifts and tummy-tucks? Aren't we supposed to be happy with what we have?*

A As usual, it's not smart to think that the Jewish people speak with a single voice about such matters. But curiously, there's less disagreement about fixing up the old bod than you might imagine, despite Maimonides's early injunctions against any surgery that is not therapeutic.

Although some Orthodox authorities continue to oppose surgery for any reason other than medical necessity, in many Orthodox circles cosmetic surgery is considered acceptable— providing that such surgery serves a positive function in the person's life, beyond sheer vanity.

So if you're considering that tummy-tuck so that you'll feel better about yourself, more satisfied with your life, some Orthodox rabbis and most Reform and Conservative rabbis will give you their blessing. But if you're doing it to glorify your body . . . forget it; it's just not the Jewish thing to do.

If that sounds like a pretty fine line, it is, which is why the subject continues to generate debate among Jewish scholars. But this lack of consensus is not necessarily a bad thing; to Sol, one of the beauties of the vast system of Jewish law is that it encourages people to *think* about their behavior instead of simply acting like mindless drones who get their ethical framework right out of *People* magazine.

⁑

Q *Is there anything Jewish in the idea of reincarnation? My wife is convinced that, if she's good, she'll come back as a cat; I think that is dumb. What does Jewish tradition have to say about this?*

A If what you mean is the idea that if you die, and then maybe wake up as Shirley MacLaine, forget it. Besides, how would *you* like to have Warren Beatty as a brother?

But a belief in a kind of reincarnation became popular with the rise of Kabbalism. In a variety of ways, the Kabbalists proposed a kind of second chance in life; each of us has a specific mission on earth, and if we blow it, we have to come back in another body to try again. If we *really* blow it, our souls may be consigned to a kind of endless wandering state—and we become, in essence, a *dybbuk,* a ghost.

Or, in another variant of the belief, misbehavior on earth can even result in reincarnation of a person into a lower life form. The idea of learning about one's previous lives and working toward the ultimate restoration of the soul became a popular theme among some Jewish groups in Eastern Europe.

Reincarnation for New Agers often represents a kind of reward for good behavior on earth; among the Kabbalists, it was more apt to be the metaphysical equivalent of being held back a grade in school.

It's also interesting to note that one of the personal failings that was supposed to result in a second pass at life was the failure to reproduce. In this, Jewish tradition is not unlike Sol's mother.

Speaking of reincarnation, Sol has always been amused by

the fact that the people who believe in reincarnation today always assume that in previous incarnations they were intriguing personalities, like Copernicus, or a jester in the court of Queen Victoria, or Nero's manicurist. You never hear a New Ager brag that he or she was descended from an illiterate sod farmer whose idea of culture was watching weeds grow.

Nor do believers in this sort of thing imagine for a moment that they will move *down* the evolutionary ladder in their next go-round.

⌇

Q *How does Judaism view astrology? Did the rabbis of old ever depend on the stars to make major decisions? What is the current view on astrology—benign nonsense or harmful witchery?*

A Sol used to believe that astrology was just fodder for those supermarket tabloids with headlines about six-headed children and space aliens who shop with American Express cards. But since it's been revealed that astrology has helped guide national policy at the highest levels, he's not so sure.

The straight answer to your question is that it's not entirely clear. On one hand, Jewish tradition includes a number of beliefs based on the positions of heavenly bodies, such as prohibition against making *kiddush* over red wine on Fridays, between the sixth and seventh hours after noon—because the sign of Mars is ascendant at that time, and red wine is . . . well, red, just like Mars.

Astrology was a matter of great controversy in the late Middle Ages. Some rabbis agreed with today's astrologers that the moment of one's birth determined his or her character because of the influence of the heavenly bodies.

Others—Maimonides was the chief critic—considered astrology the science of fools.

If you need proof that astrology was once an accepted part of Jewish life, consider what you say at every bar mitzvah and wedding: mazel tov, which literally means, "may your constellation be a good one," according to the *Encyclopedia Judaica.*

Remember, too, that in the old days, there was not much of a line between astronomers and astrologers. Astrology was considered a legitimate science; serious thinkers speculated about the influence of the stars on everyday life.

In more modern times, Orthodox thinkers have tended to reject the stars and planets as active forces in human life, because such a belief would deny the preeminence of God.

So in the rabbinic tradition, there may be connections between the stars and events on earth—but only as an expression of divine disposition, not as an active force in everyday human affairs. So if you're Jewish, you may not want to use astrology to decide the best time to apply for a job, or sign an INF treaty.

By the way, what's *your* sign?

Q *If it is determined that computers have souls, will the rabbis rule that they're Jewish? If so, can they join the B'nai B'rith?*

A Sol put your question to one Conservative rabbi of his acquaintance, whose response should go down as one of the most pithy in the somewhat long-winded annals of rabbinic rulings: "If my grandmother had wheels," this rabbi said, "she'd be a bus."

Get it? Computers, by definition, don't have souls, because they are not people. No matter how smart your IBM gets, and no matter how far data-processing engineers push the science of "artificial intelligence," that computer of yours can never have a soul. Not even if it learns all by itself to sing James Brown songs.

Therefore, it can not become Jewish. Besides, it would look pretty strange in a crocheted yarmulke.

Can they join B'nai B'rith? From what Sol hears, the big

international Jewish organization could use a few more members, so that may be within the realm of possibility.

Q *If a pious man keyed the Torah into a computer, what would he have to do to treat the machine in accordance with Jewish law?*

A You're missing the point here. The real question is this: since your computer screen goes blank every time you shut the darned thing off, wouldn't you be, in effect, erasing the name of God if you tried to put the Torah onto your trusty Mac?

Well, Orthodox rabbis may look like they're behind the times, but they're no slouches when it comes to modern technology; a lot of these guys know more about RAM chips and 16-bit processors than *you* do.

Many rabbis have looked at this question of electronic communications, and while the issue is far from settled, there is a general feeling that things like computers and word processors, which deal in mere electronic representations of words, are "transparent" when it comes to such regulations.

So what a scribe puts on paper is enduring; one of the reasons for never writing the name of God is to avoid erasing it. What goes onto your computer lacks the same quality of reality, and is therefore something you shouldn't be too concerned about.

In the interests of thoroughness, Sol should emphasize that the issue of transience in electronic recording is still a hot topic in halachic circles. Sol suggests you play it safe and consult your own rabbi.

Q *What is the Jewish position on organ transplants? Usually the organs involved come from dead people—and Jews, I know, have strict prohibitions against desecrating the dead, even to the extent of rejecting autopsies.*

A. Never fear, the rabbinic establishment is hard at work thrashing out the moral maze created by modern slice-and-dice medicine. With any luck, they'll arrive at some kind of consensus in about one hundred years.

And although some of these rabbinic disputations might sound picky to ordinary folks, Sol, for one, is glad that *someone* is asking basic ethical questions about these astounding new technologies.

In general, the transplantation issue reflects a tension between the priority placed on saving lives—even when the process involves things like violating Sabbath laws—and some very basic rules about death.

Many rabbis argue that the idea of getting a new heart or kidney is acceptable, but only if it is a matter of absolute medical necessity. None of these cosmetic heart transplants for Jews, no siree. It doesn't particularly matter if the organ comes from a Jew or a non-Jew.

But there *are* vexing ethical problems that the rabbis are still working on. For example, how do we determine the moment of the donor's death? More and more, the secular world defines death in terms of an absence of brain waves on an electronic machine; the traditional Jewish definition involves an absence of breathing and heartbeat.

So consider this scenario: a heart donor is brain-dead, but his heart is kept beating through artificial means until just before the transplant operation. According to the Jewish way of looking at things, wouldn't the surgeon then be killing the donor?

Some Orthodox scholars suggest that the halachic definition of death should be modified to take into account artificial means of keeping the heart beating, something unknown in Talmudic times. Others maintain that tampering with basically sound Jewish laws could open up a Pandora's box. Makes the old head swim, doesn't it?

Some Orthodox people also object to organ transplants because of the mutilation of the donor, and because the body is consequently buried without all its parts. And many people suggest that Jews who want to donate their organs must do so directly, and not through an organ bank, since there must be a clear connection between the donor and the person whose life is being saved.

Sol is no rabbi, and this is incredibly complicated stuff. Suffice it to say that Jewish practice takes a cautious approach when it comes to proclaiming people dead, and a compassionate one in bending the rules a little to save lives. But as they say, the jury is out—at least for the very Orthodox, who take these kinds of questions very seriously.

Q *Dear Sol: I wear contact lenses. Recently I noticed that the enzyme solution I use to treat them is made with pig fat. Is this a violation of Jewish law? Do I need to change to specs?*

A Fat on your *eyes?* Sol thinks he is going to be sick.

But if it's *Halachah* you're worried about, you can bathe your contacts to your heart's delight. Prohibitions against the meat of the swine do not apply to products that you rub on

your body. The only things that count when it comes to those nasty critters is the stuff you might eat.

If products derived from swine were a halachic problem, a lot of us would be looking for new soaps, skin moisturizers, and the like. Modern chemistry has given a whole new meaning to the phrase "bringing home the bacon."

Back Roads and Side Trips Through Jewish History

Q *Who was the most famous Jewish criminal of all time?*
A Although the Jewish community has not exactly been known for its bad guys, when it does produce them, it produces doozies.

In the sheer evil category, you'd have to give high marks to Nathan Leopold and Richard Loeb—the rich Jewish young men from Chicago who conducted an experiment in Nietzschean philosophy by abducting and killing the young son of a wealthy neighbor.

Loeb, whose father was a top executive of Sears Roebuck, subsequently died in prison; Leopold was paroled after 33 years in the slammer, and went on to write a book.

The Leopold-Loeb story had some interesting sidebars. One friend of both boys was Meyer Levin, the prominent Jewish author who won fame and fortune with his superb novel about the case, *Compulsion*. Another friend was Will Gier, a young drama student at the University of Chicago who went on to change his name to Geer—and play the grandfather on "The Waltons."

※

Q *Dear Sol: A while back, you referred to the Leopold and Loeb murder case. I was fascinated by your answer, because I remember my parents talking about it. What I was wondering was this: were these boys from religious families? Did they go to Jewish schools?*

A Sol certainly hopes your question is not yet another sly plug for Jewish day schools.

As you no doubt surmised, Nathan Leopold and Richard Loeb weren't exactly yeshiva boys. Both were the scions of wealthy, highly assimilated Jewish families on Chicago's South Side, members of the German-Jewish elite.

Nathan Leopold, especially, was a kind of religious experimenter. As a child, he undertook his own comprehensive study of religion—by getting the family chauffeur to drive him to different churches on Sunday mornings so he could sample from the Christian smorgasbord.

Despite this experimentation, there is no evidence that Leopold cared much about any religion. At his trial, he held forth on his philosophy, which included a strong dose of atheism.

During his decades in jail, he did participate in religious activities among the Jewish prisoners—but according to at least one biographer, he did so simply to escape the boredom of prison life and to get special meals.

As for your parents talking about the case, that's not surprising. In 1924, when Leopold and Loeb did their dastardly deed, the case was a national sensation for many months. And for the Jewish community, it was a prolonged nightmare; it is difficult today to understand the trauma that the case caused the nervous Jewish community back then.

※

Q *Someone told me that there was once a plan to create a Jewish homeland right here in the U.S. of A. Is this true, and could Baltimore have been the projected site? What happened to the plan? Was it some kind of scam, like a time-share?*

A Baltimore is many things to many people, but a Jewish homeland it ain't.

The story to which you refer involved a flamboyant guy named Mordecai Noah, the leading Jewish politician of his day—which happened to be the early decades of the nineteenth century. Noah, who served as American consul in Tunis back in the early 1800s, had a grand Zionist vision before Theodor Herzl was even a twinkle in his parents' eyes: a Jewish homeland on a tract of land near Buffalo, New York, a place with all the climatic appeal of the North Pole.

Noah, according to historian Arthur Hertzberg, even gave himself a job in the proposed colony—"high sheriff of the Jews," and picked a name for his mini-state: Ararat, after the mountain where Noah's Ark presumably struck dry land.

Noah also had the idea that the American Indians were descended from the Ten Tribes, not an unheard of idea even today. According to Hertzberg, Ararat would be the first step in uniting the Indians with their Jewish brethren.

Alas, Noah's plans for a Jewish homeland did not trigger an exodus to upstate New York. The rest of the story is well known: Jews today have to make do with a homeland on the sunny Mediterranean, instead of icebound upstate New York. As for Noah, he seemed unaffected by this silly idea; later in his life, he promoted a plan to buy Syria for a Jewish homeland.

Q *Does anybody know what Albert Einstein received as presents for his bar mitzvah? I mean, did he get slide rules and other scientific things that helped him develop his intellect, or*

did he have to make due with dictionaries and dumb pens, like the rest of us?

A Very funny. Uncle Albert, who has become the closest thing to a Jewish saint in some circles, received none of the above mentioned bar mitzvah gifts for the simple reason that he never had a bar mitzvah.

The matter of Einstein's religious practices remains a sore point with the more Orthodox among us. As a child, he was sent to a Catholic school by his thoroughly assimilated parents; later, while he was spouting incomprehensible theories and modeling the hair style that would later be used with such great effect in *The Bride of Frankenstein,* his theology evolved in the direction of what might today be called humanistic Judaism.

On the other side of the coin, Einstein was a committed Zionist, dating back to the time he won the Nobel Prize in 1921. Like many of the early Zionists, he emphasized the idea of living peacefully with Israel's Arab neighbors—and he argued forcefully against the idea of a "narrow nationalism" in the Jewish state, positions that might well place him in the Peace Now camp, if he were alive today.

If he were alive today, he might also have finally learned how to comb his hair.

Q *I had a teacher once who insisted that U.S. Grant was the most anti-Semitic president in the history of this country. Is this true? What did he say or do?*

A Grant, never much of a favorite with historians, had his share of problems with the Jewish community as well. Whether this was anti-Semitism or merely the same incompetence for which his administration was later renowned, Sol would not hazard a guess.

The story involves Grant's infamous Order Number 11, which he issued in 1862 when he commanded parts of Kentucky, Tennessee, and Mississippi.

Despite the bitter Civil War, there was a flourishing trade in cotton and medical supplies between North and South, and some of it was conducted by Jews—facts that drove the high-strung general right up a tree.

In response, Grant issued his order, which began with these memorable lines:

"The Jews, as a class violating every regulation of trade established by the Treasury Department and also Department Orders, are hereby expelled from the Department within 24 hours from receipt of this order."

The "Department," in case you missed the point, was the entire area under Grant's jurisdiction.

Incensed Jews eventually brought their case straight to Abe Lincoln, who ordered it to be rescinded.

Grant's motives will never be known; there was no *National Enquirer* in those days to tell us what people really thought. The language of his order speaks for itself. On the other hand, Grant appointed a number of Jews to high-level positions when he moved to the White House.

※

Q *Who started those rumors that Jews need Christian blood for their Passover matzah? And isn't it stupid to begin with, since matzah isn't red?*

A You know it and I know it, bubbe. But human ignorance is infinite; absolutely idiotic ideas apparently have just as good a chance of sticking around for centuries as the really good ones.

In this latter category we have the blood-libel myth, the meat and potatoes of anti-Semites throughout the ages.

The idea that Jews murder Christians to obtain blood for various rituals originated in Greek times, during the period of tremendous tension between Hellenism and Judaism. The idea back then was that Jews would capture a Greek, fatten him up, and then kill him for ritual purposes.

Like so many ideas born of that turbulent era, the blood-libel myth kept coming back over the centuries. It found especially fertile soil in seventeenth-century Eastern Europe.

The idea of blood as an essential ingredient of Passover matzah was given a boost by the fact that Passover and Easter frequently overlap—and by general ignorance of the fairly arcane rituals of Jewish life.

Alas, the idea is alive even today; in recent years, blood-libel accusations have hovered around the edges of several missing-child cases.

🗯

Q *Sol, okay, everybody knows that circumcision has been a requirement for male Jews since Biblical days. But in view of the current medical debate over the practice, I was wondering: was there ever any serious opposition to circumcision?*

A You bet. Sol has heard of precious few eight-day-old boys who go the *mohel* full of enthusiasm.

Or were you referring to organized opposition to circumcision within the Jewish community? On that score, the opinion on circumcision has been remarkably consistent over the centuries. Only a few times in Jewish history did movements arise to abolish the practice—and these didn't exactly catch on.

For example, the "Society of the Friends of Reform," an early German offshoot of the Reform movement, argued against circumcision, citing arguments like the fact that Moses didn't have his own son circumcised.

But these kinds of arguments did not inflame the Jewish masses; in fact, they fell flat. In modern times, of course, the question has been pretty much moot in most Western nations as the prevailing medical wisdom called for circumcision for *every* male infant.

Recently, sentiment against routine circumcision has grown in the non-Jewish world, because of the widespread belief that the procedure inflicts unnecessary pain on the infant without providing any medical benefits. Orthodox Jews will continue to regard the practice as a basic commandment: case closed. But for more secularized Jews, the matter may again generate some debate.

Q *Sol, is it true that Hebrew came within a hair's breadth of becoming the official language of the United Stages?*

A "Hair's breadth" may be overstating things a little (until he became an Answer Man, Sol used to think the expression was "hare's breath"), but the shocking truth is, there was a vigorous movement during the Revolutionary War that wanted to write the Constitution from right to left.

Back then, everything smacking of British influence was suspect—including the language. Interestingly, this aversion continued well into the twentieth century; before the First World War, politicians regularly got mileage out of Britain-bashing, much as some of today's pols flail away at Secular Humanists.

Anyway, many colonists regarded Hebrew as the ideal language for the American democratic experiment. Several members of the First Congress took this view, though they were never able to sell the idea to their colleagues, who were probably having a hard enough time with English.

And back in Colonial days, a knowledge of Hebrew was considered essential for the educated person.

Q *Has there ever been a Jewish pope? Don't laugh; I heard something about this when I was a kid.*

A Ach, the questions Answer Men get asked.

When Sol was young, his mother liked to insist that there was no field of endeavor a Jew couldn't pursue. Sol suspects she had something more modest than the papacy in mind, like the presidency, maybe.

Well, there *was* a Jewish pope, if you want to stretch the

definition somewhat. He was Anacletus II, great-grandson of a Jewish businessman named Baruch, and he was elected to the papacy in 1130.

Unfortunately for him, he wasn't the only one to get the nod; a few hours before his election by part of the College of Cardinals, the *rest* of the cardinals elected the man who became Innocent II. Some of the dissension over the election was the result of anti-Semitism, even though Anacletus wasn't exactly a bright beacon of Judaism.

Thus a schism was formed, not entirely unlike the coalition governments that seem so popular in Jerusalem. It seems that Anacletus got the bum's rush from the history books; little asterisks in lists of the popes list him as an "antipope," for reasons that may have been more political that theological.

Q *Jimmy Swaggart, Oral Roberts—there sure are a lot of embarrassing folks preaching for Christians. Human nature being what it is, why don't there seem to be any such holy embarrassments in the Jewish world?*

A Sol hates to be the source of disillusionment, but there have been Jewish religious snake-oil salesmen who make Jim Bakker look like a man of deep piety.

You doubt Uncle Sol's word? Just read up a little about Shabbatai Zevi, the False Messiah who whipped European and Asian Jewry into an apocalyptic froth back in the 1660s. Zevi was only the most famous of a long line of messianic pretenders.

By the way, Zevi, who later converted to Islam, married a woman with a dubious reputation; compared to her, Tammy Faye is a model of modesty and good taste.

Modern Judaism does seem less prone to these sorts of charlatans. Jews today tend to be skeptical about the cult of personality; there's a recognition of human frailty that makes it tough for Jewish leaders to get away with pretenses of perfection. It's no accident that Judaism does not have saints.

And Judaism generally assumes that prophecy ceased with Malachi; a rabbi who got on television and announced that God had told him to raise millions of dollars for a religious theme park would be hooted right off the air.

Also, Jewish leaders are tied to the halachic tradition; it's not easy to attract the Jewish masses with some new formulation that departs radically from that ancient tradition.

With the exception of some Chasidim, Jews tend to venerate their rabbis as teachers, not as seers or intermediaries.

Q *Who was the first Jewish congressman? Senator? Cabinet member?*

A It is commonly thought that the first Jew in both the House and Senate was one man—David Levy Yulee—who represented Florida first in the House (1841–1845) and then in the Senate (1845–1851 and 1855–1861).

Actually, Yulee, whose name reminds Sol of the kind of soft drink you can buy only at rural gas stations in the Deep South, had a strange ethnic heritage. His grandfather was Portuguese, his grandmother was an English Jew, and his father was described as a "religious socialist," an exotic species now considered extinct.

Yulee was apparently a Jew by descent, not practice; records show he was buried as a Presbyterian. He is best remembered for his passionate advocacy of iron ships, which is probably why schoolchildren don't learn his name along with Franklin's and Jefferson's.

Interestingly, just under half of the Jews who have ever served in the Senate are there right now. Currently, there are seven Jewish senators; all told, there have only been 16 or so.

As for the first Jewish cabinet member, that didn't occur until 1908, when Oscar S. Straus worked as secretary of Commerce and Labor under Teddy Roosevelt. No, Straus didn't hold the Commerce job by day, and moonlight at

Labor on the second shift; prior to 1913, Commerce and Labor were a single department.

Straus, a lawyer, diplomat, and philanthropist, wrote extensively on an issue that still has a special meaning to Jewish politicians—religious liberty. Because he served presidents of both parties, he is remembered as one of the first "career diplomats."

※

Q *Sol, I was wondering about something I heard recently. I am very opposed to smoking. But I heard that Jews control a major portion of the tobacco industry today. How did this shameful situation come about?*

A Sorry to be the bearer of bad tidings, but Jews have traditionally had a hand in the killer weed trade—and this continues even in the era of those pesky "Surgeon General's Warnings" that seem to work about as well as speed-limit signs and President Gerald Ford's "Whip Inflation Now" buttons, the thinking man's answer to inflation.

Tobacco was brought to Europe from the New World by Christopher Columbus, and almost immediately Marranos took a hand in its cultivation, processing, and sale—not to mention its use.

In the early days, tobacco was essentially a cottage industry; through the 1700s and 1800s, it was a major source of income for Jews in Eastern Europe.

And those Jews took their trade with them when they emigrated to the United States—bringing tobacco full circle, in a sense. In the early days of this century, the tobacco industry was the second largest employer of Jews—after the garment industry.

Today, alas, the process continues. But tobacco is no longer a cottage industry; it's a multi-billion-dollar enterprise, controlled by economic giants like the Loews Corporation. When conglomerates began to take over the tobacco companies, Jewish involvement in the industry increased significantly—so much so that some Jewish anti-smoking crusaders are making a great clamor about the ethics of the killer weed trade.

Anti-Semites, of course, will gleefully detect sinister conspiracies in all this. Sorry, guys: while Sol is second to none in his anti-smoking passions, it is evident to him that the rising Jewish presence in the industry has more to do with the changing nature of American big business than with an insidious Jewish plot to give the rest of the world emphysema.

⚶

Q *Sol, is there any place in this country named after a Jew?*

A A long time ago, Bernard Postal, a writer with nothing better to do, compiled a list of such places, a veritable travelogue of places that read like a roster for the local *shul*.

What he came up with was a grand total of 92 place-names with obviously Jewish origins. Unfortunately, there were no big cities on the list; the most Jews managed to attain was a rural county or two, and a long list of burgs of the wide-bend-in-the-road variety.

At least 34 states, he reported, have places with Jewish names; about one-third of these places are in the South. For those really into trivia, these 92 places contain some 230,000 souls. But, being small towns without good delis, almost no Jews live in them.

The biggest towns named after Jews? You guessed it: Levittown, Pennsylvania and Levittown, New York, the post-war developments that gave birth to the whole idea of urban sprawl.

You may also be interested to know that there's a Levy County in Florida and a town of Levy in New Mexico. There's a Goldman, Arkansas, and a Kahnville in Mississippi, not to mention Kaplan, Louisiana—a rice town, according to the author, whatever that is.

⚶

Q *Dear Sol: I am confused about Jewish names. I admit it: most of what I know about Judaism, I learned from* Exodus. *But at least I know that Jews in the distant past didn't have last names.*

Yet everyone knows there is a long list of characteristically Jewish surnames, like Cohen or Kaplan. Now explain to me: if Jews traditionally lacked surnames, why are there so many traditional Jewish surnames today?

A Sol is frequently amazed at the number of American Jews who seem to think that Leon Uris was the author of one of the books of the Bible. Sol is no literary critic, but he doubts that the Uris version of *Exodus* will have the staying power of the original. If you want conclusive proof, look at the film version; any story that could feature Paul Newman as a sabra has what you might call serious credibility problems.

But on to business. You are right in that it wasn't until the 1700s that Jews began to use last names, as distinct from constructions that indicated their paternity, as in "Joseph ben Meyer," Joseph, son of Meyer.

Just in case you didn't notice, there's an interesting double standard at work here. Kids in those days were named as the sons or daughters of fathers. Yet Judaism is handed down through the matrilineal line. Was this blatant sexism, or just a concession to fathers, who, after all, didn't count for beans when it came to determining the Jewish identity of their offspring? Sol will not hazard a guess.

In any case, during the eighteenth century, many European countries passed regulations requiring Jews to take last names, an effort to promote the integration of Jews into the broader culture.

So, many Jews took what was at hand and created surnames for themselves. Hymie ben Meyer, Hymie the son of Meyer, might have renamed himself "Hymie Meyerson." Some Jews took on the names of their places of residence; a whole bunch of Jews living in Berlin became Berliner. Luckily for Jewish culture, this phenomenon did not take place in

Truth or Consequences, New Mexico. And some Jews took on names having to do with their professions, as in Goldsmith.

And many Jews took on names based on their religious status; hence Cohen and Levy and the infinite number of variations on that theme.

Q *Are the American Indians really one of the Ten Lost Tribes? How about the Japanese? The Eskimos? Who or what were the Ten Lost Tribes, anyway? Weren't they members of AAA, and didn't they leave with a map?*

A You left out cab drivers in New York, just about the only ethnic group not believed at one time or another to be one of the long-lost tribes of Israel.

One of the most enduring hobbies through the ages has been speculating about the modern descendants of these folks, the 27,000 or so northern Israelites taken into exile by the Assyrians in the eighth century B.C.E.

It was never really clear what happened to them. But the event was recorded in the Bible—and thus provided the raw materials for an endless number of crackpots with exotic theories about their eventual destination. Included on the long list of possible Lost Tribes peoples are certain tribes in Afghanistan, the Yoruba tribe in Nigeria, the Hindus, the Falashas, and—believe it or not—the Anglo-Saxons.

A guy named Cadillac helped popularize the theory that the American Indians were the descendants of the Lost Tribes. His reasoning had to do with nose-piercing ceremonies and alleged similarities in language between the Indians in Michigan and the ancient Hebrews.

To give you an idea of how strange this guy was, he also believed Detroit might someday be a halfway livable city. For such contributions to American culture, he was rewarded with a line of luxury cars named after him.

Clearly, Cadillac's anthropology was just about as bad as

his judgment about cities. Still, the American Indian theory keeps turning up, like a bad penny.

The question of the Lost Tribes' fate would be a mere historical oddity, were it not for the fact that their exile split apart the Jewish nation. According to prophecies accepted by both Christianity and Orthodox Jewry, the nation must once again be united before the Messiah can come—for the second time or the first, depending on your religion.

And how can the nation be restored, when nobody knows who in the blazes these people are?

Sol personally recommends the theory that the Japanese are the descendants of the Lost Tribes. Think of it: millions of them could make *aliyah,* and the desert would bloom with Honda factories and sushi bars. After a few years of this, Israel would be rolling in shekels, and could join her Arab neighbors and Japan in buying up just about every business worth buying in the United States.

And then, they could give *us* foreign aid.

Q *Did George Washington have any Jewish friends?*

A Sorry, Sol has plenty of connections, but he is not in direct contact with the old boy himself.

The available evidence on Washington's relations with Jews is sketchy. One historian noted that Washington once spent a night in the home of a Philadelphia Jew, Isaac Franks. There is no record of whether George enjoyed his stay, or sent a thank-you note.

In his landmark book *The Jews in America,* Rabbi Arthur Hertzberg cited Washington's first official contact with the small American Jewish community—letters from the six synagogues congratulating the president on his election. Washington was probably not upset that only six bothered to write; at that time, there *were* only six synagogues in the new nation.

Washington replied cordially, but Hertzberg noted that

there is no evidence that Washington was given much to thinking about this tiny minority. He had enough to worry about, like finding powder for his wig once commerce with England was interrupted by the Revolution.

᙭

Q *Are there any characteristically Jewish musical instruments?*

A You mean besides synthesizers that can play only "Moon River" and "Hava Nagila" at Jewish weddings?

If you want to go back to Biblical days, probably the instrument most associated with Jews was the *kinnor,* not exactly something the Bad Brains might use today in a music video.

It was this instrument—a kind of lyre, with a curved frame and up to ten strings—that was called "King David's Harp," even though, technically, it was not a harp at all.

You want to know what a *kinnor* looks like? Watch old "Star Trek" episodes. In several, Mr. Spock, possibly the only Jew on the planet Vulcan, played an instrument that looks similar to the Biblical *kinnor.*

᙭

Q *Did any Jews fight for the Confederacy in the Civil War?*

A Abe Lincoln may have been the Great Emancipator, but to Lewis Leon, a dry-goods clerk from North Carolina who volunteered to fight for the Confederacy in the early days of the conflict, he was the enemy.

Fortunately for historians, Leon kept a diary during his war service. Unfortunately, he provides little insight into what it must have been like to be one of a relative handful of Jews in the middle of the Confederate Army.

But Leon does refer to the Jewish holidays, and to a proclamation by General Robert E. Lee granting a furlough to every "Israelite" soldier to go to Richmond for High Holiday services.

Excerpts from Leon's diary can be found in *A Documentary History of the Jews in the United States,* edited by Morris U. Schappes.

On the other side of the lines, there were a number of Jews fighting for the Union, including at least one Jewish company. Chicago was able to muster a company of 96 men in the Concordia Guards. The so-called Israelite Company saw heavy action at such places as Chancellorsville and Gettysburg.

According to some estimates there were more than 5,000 Jews serving in the Union Army, including a number of officers.

Since we're on the topic of Jews in the Civil War, let's not forget Judah Philip Benjamin, who served as secretary of state in the Confederate government.

⁂

Q *Why did so many Jewish immigrants stay in New York? I mean, these were primarily rural and small-town people from the* shtetl; *you'd think they'd have been happier in Iowa or Illinois than in Manhattan. Was it that New York was particularly tolerant of Jews?*

A It depends. If you go back far enough in New York history, the Big Apple—then just a little seed, maybe—began with a distinctly anti-Jewish bias.

Peter Stuyvesant, director of the West India Company in New Amsterdam, fought hard to expel the first group of hopeful Jewish immigrants who arrived in 1654, refugees from Portugal. Among other things, Stuyvesant referred to Jews as "the deceitful race—such hateful enemies and blasphemers in the name of Christ."

Despite Stuyvesant's bigotry, Jewish life took root in New York for a number of reasons. New York, to begin with, was where almost all of them washed up.

Moreover, it was a cosmopolitan city with the kinds of industries that gobbled up—exploited might be a better word for it—newly arrived immigrants.

Jews, who hit these shores already possessing many of the skills that were desperately needed by the industrial revolution underway in the United States, were able to rise in fields like the garment industry and the cigar-making business, therefore cementing the bond to New York.

Also, the communal structure that Jews built in those early years proved a powerful incentive for permanent residence. It's hard to picture what a lot of these guys would have done in Mineral Point, Wisconsin: no jobs, no shuls, and a lot of locals looking at them like they were from the planet Neptune.

Q *Who was the most famous Jewish cowboy of all time?*
A Sol hates to rain on your parade, but this is one of those questions that keeps trivia column writers in business. Who really *cares* about Jewish cowboys? Why don't people ask interesting questions, like, "How did they keep kosher out there where the buffalo roam?"

But it *is* interesting to Sol that Wyatt Earp, the rogue law officer whose image was cleaned up for his television show, married a Jewish woman. According to the *Jewish Almanac*, Josephine Sarah Marcus, better known as Sadie, married the lawman sometime around 1880 and lived happily ever after. What's more, Ms. Earp's story was told in a made-for-TV movie a few years ago—and the part of this pioneer in Jewish achievement was played by Marie Osmond, who is about as Jewish as Mother Teresa.

And no, there's not a lick of truth to the rumor that Wild Bill Hickok was a yeshiva graduate who chucked it all for the wide-open spaces.

Q *Is the image of the Wandering Jew a Jewish image? And how did a plant get that name, for crying out loud?*

A Wrong religion, bubbe. In the Middle Ages, the story was told that a Jewish cobbler in Jerusalem taunted Jesus on the way to his crucifixion. As a result, he was condemned to live forever in exile, until Christ's return.

The legend proved a durable and remarkably adaptable one; over and over again, especially in the Middle Ages, rumors spread of some new appearance of the mythical character. The Wandering Jew figures prominently in English balladry; it was a popular image in German and French literature.

In more recent centuries, the legend has come to apply more to Jews in general. Anti-Semites have used the image to bolster their idea of a people damned by their obduracy; those of a more tolerant bent have used the Wandering Jew as a symbol of the trials and tribulations of a people in exile.

In botany, the term refers to the plants *Zebrina pendula* and *Tradescantia fluminensis*, known for their trailing, fast-growing qualities, which might suggest the image of "wandering" to a person with a few beers under his belt. The term was first applied to the plant in England—where the image of the Wandering Jew was particularly popular.

You'll be enchanted to know that there's something also known as the "wandering of the poles." But, alas, it has to do with magnetism, not ethnicity.

THREE

A Peculiar People
Strange Jewish Facts, Strange Jews

Q *Why are there so few Jewish hunters?*
A What, you just noticed a lack of gun-toting guys in 4x4 pickups, wearing camouflage *kippah?*

There are two basic reasons for this phenomenon. The first is demographic; Jews in this country are by and large urban creatures, while the hunting population draws disproportionately from the rural and small town environment. Young boys in Brooklyn are more likely to study Talmud with Abba than tramp through the woods shooting animals and occasional passersby.

Secondly, there are religious factors at work here. Observant Jews can't eat the meat from animals killed in the wild, unless the killing is done by a qualified *shochet* according to the ritual guidelines. The hills and dales of America are not exactly teaming with ritual slaughterers.

And if the meat is forbidden, the killing becomes purely a matter of sport—a practice frowned upon in Jewish tradition.

A story is told about Moses Montefiore, the Jewish Lord Mayor of London in the 1800s. According to custom, the King or Queen would give the mayor one deer a year. When Montefiore contemplated *his* gift, he did the only kosher thing; he took a *shochet* to Richmond Park, and had the deer butchered according to Jewish law.

As for hunting in this day and age, Sol suggests a more humane sport, like joining the Book-of-the-Month Club.

Q *Dear Sol: I have a number of Orthodox friends, and I have noticed that none of them has much of an interest in exercising. No jogging, no racquetball, no invigorating hours on an exercise bike. Is this a matter of Jewish religion,*

culture, or custom? Don't Orthodox Jews approve of the health-oriented life-style?

A You find exercise bikes invigorating? You're probably also the kind of person who gets rapturous every time you use an electric can opener.

There's nothing in Jewish law prohibiting good, healthy exercise; over and over again, Jews are commanded to take good care of their bodies.

But the fetish that has made Jane Fonda one of America's five leading industries evokes some strong images from the Jewish past, and raises the kind of moral questions that keep the rabbinate from being a dull profession.

Specifically, some Orthodox Jews object to the excessive emphasis on body image—one of the bones of contention between the Jews and the Greeks in the days of Antiochus IV. This conflict between the Greek emphasis on the physical and the Jewish emphasis on the moral and spiritual has somehow survived the passing of the centuries, and continues to play a big role in Orthodox Jewish thinking.

On the other end of the denominational spectrum, Sol knows at least one Reform rabbi who runs marathons, and there is no lack of Jews of various persuasions pumping iron or walking treadmills like high-tech hamsters. For these Jews, the health benefits—and, let's be honest, the benefits of looking good in their new clothes—outweigh the historical uneasiness with the Hellenizing influence.

Personally, Sol could never see the thrill of running up and down the street while encased in one of those polyester sausage-casing running outfits. Sol prefers aerobic reading.

※

Note to Readers:
In the column above, Sol tackled the issue of why Orthodox Jews do not seem to be enthusiastic participants in the exercise boom. In that column, Sol recklessly implied that there was little in Jewish tradition discouraging vigorous exercise.

Well, Sol quickly heard from Rabbi Sheldon Ezring of the Temple Society of Concord in Syracuse, New York. Ezring, besides being a Reform rabbi, is a marathon runner and an all-around great guy.

But he was not impressed with Sol's answer on Jewish resistance to good, healthy exercise.

"My research shows a totally negative attitude toward aerobic sports or athletics in any form in Jewish tradition," Ezring writes. He also pointed out that the Talmud blames the destruction of the Temple on boys playing ball on Shabbat and on Greco-Roman nakedness in sport; attitudes like these generated an antagonism to athletics that continues to this day, in the rabbi's view.

Some noted rabbis in the last century, Ezring said, tried to promote physical fitness, but generally, their pronouncements were ignored by the Orthodox community.

"Only a couple of people, like Maimonides, seem to be supportive," the rabbi writes. "Well, what can you do?"

Sol thanks Rabbi Ezring, and hopes his sneakers don't wear out.

⁂

Q *Can Jews become sumo wrestlers?*

A Sol confesses to a certain ignorance of the arcane sport of sumo wrestling, not to mention a degree of distaste. No doubt this is a purely cultural bias; to the Japanese, this sport is a thing of special grace and beauty.

That being said, there are several answers to your question. Jews *have* been professional wrestlers in this country, they *can* get fat, and some are even susceptible to ridiculous garb.

But the most secular American Jew probably shares a certain repugnance toward the display of so much human blubber; despite the almost universal tendency to excess poundage, to the American eye, thin is beautiful, fat is not.

And the more Orthodox among us have always esteemed modesty in dress, as well as moderation in one's habits—

qualities that must be regarded as almost sinful by these Japanese behemoths.

Are you considering a change in this direction for yourself? Sol counsels some interesting psychotherapy and a lifetime membership at Weight Watchers.

Q *There are Jewish groups for everything, so I was wondering: are there Jewish nudist colonies, too? And what does Jewish law have to say about this kind of behavior?*

A Are you asking out of pure intellectual curiosity, bubbe? Or are you thinking of baring your *pupik* to a thoroughly apathetic world?

Jewish law takes a dim view of such things as nudist colonies. Modesty in dress is clearly prescribed in *Halachah*, and it would be pretty curious logic to suggest that nudist colonies represent even the faintest shred of modesty.

This, of course, doesn't mean that such things as Jewish

nudist colonies do not exist. But this is a family column, bubbe; if it's referrals you're looking for, look somewhere else.

Note to Readers:

When Sol recklessly bared the question of Jewish nudist colonies, he was almost immediately called on the carpet by Dr. Leonard Lehrman, a New York pianist, conductor, and composer who is active in the "naturist" movement. What follows are excerpts from Dr. Lehrman's letter.

Dear Sol:

The query re "Jewish nudist colonies," to which you so flippantly replied in your column, deserves, I think, a more thoughtful response.

First of all, the term "nudist colony" is a bit archaic. The preferred term among most persons today practicing clothing-optional life-styles (of which there are millions, worldwide) is "naturism," and the areas where they congregate are generally beaches or resorts, not "colonies."

Secondly, there certainly are, or have been, such areas in Israel. One, near the Egyptian border, was immortalized in a song by the folksinger Mark Levy. I don't know of any specifically Jewish naturist groups in the United States. But there are "special interest groups" among naturists in dozens of areas, so why not Judaism? Perhaps your inquirer would be interested in starting one.

Lehrman goes on to describe the First International Naturist Opera Workshop in France, where three of the four professional musicians participating were American Jews. And he countered the argument that Judaism demands modesty:

Your invocation of *Halachah* as prescribing modesty is unconvincing to any except perhaps the most Orthodox of

Jews, who still believe that women should be invisible to men who are praying, and that the sound of a woman's singing voice is too lascivious to be heard by a man. As Paul M. Bowman has pointed out, "There is no Biblical condemnation of the uncovered human body; there *are* a number of references that definitely do not condemn public nudity, and one where God actually commanded a prophet to go naked for three years."

You get the idea. Sol sticks by his original answer; although there are always exceptions to the rule, most religious Jews from all three major branches take a dim view of public nudity.

But hey, if it works for you, Dr. Lehrman, mazel tov. And Sol can just imagine that opera workshop; talk about your vibrato.

Q *Why is klezmer music sometimes called Jewish jazz?*
A The recent renaissance of klezmer music is a real relief for a community that once considered vaguely Yiddishized versions of "Moon River" *de rigueur* for weddings and bar mitzvah parties.

Klezmorim were informal musical groups in Jewish communities throughout Eastern Europe. No Jewish wedding in the *shtetl* was complete without a band of shabby *klezmorim,* with their wailing clarinets and brass and such musical oddities as the *tsimbalom,* a close cousin of the American hammered dulcimer. More often than not, the musicians were paid in food and booze, not money.

The "Jewish jazz" appellation derives from the fact that the music was highly improvisational; like most street musicians, *klezmorim* didn't bother with things like musical notation and strict arrangements.

In fact, klezmer music had its origin in the Middle Ages, when jazz was but a distant twinkle in mankind's eye. It began with itinerant Jewish musicians who roamed from Bohemia to Lithuania and Poland; along the way, they picked up musical elements from Hungary, Romania, Russia, and just about every other culture in Eastern Europe.

By the way, the word "klezmer" derives from the Hebrew word for "musical instruments," with a later stop in Yiddish, where it referred to "itinerant musicians."

Q *Sol, is an abnormally high percentage of the legal profession Jewish? It seems to me that Jews have enough bad press without this blight.*

A Sol will refrain from cheap lawyer jokes, like this one: Question: what do you have when you have a lawyer up to his neck in sand? Answer: not enough sand.

The plain fact is, nobody has collected data on Jews in this darkest of professions. Even so eminent a body as the International Association of Jewish Lawyers and Jurists would not venture so much as a guess.

One expert, a well-known lawyer himself, suggested that

the proportion of Jews in the legal profession is "somewhat higher" than the proportion of Jews in the general population.

This authority suggested that the slight tendency towards barristerism is actually declining, due to the fact that in the last couple of decades, new professions have opened up for Jews—like engineering and finance. A generation ago, medical schools still had "Jewish quotas," and few Jews could be found in the upper echelons of Wall Street; now, with greatly enhanced access to these high-paying jobs, law is no longer one of very few routes to affluence open to ambitious young Jews.

Q *Why do Jews have an aversion to dogs?*

A Sol, one of your more objective Answer Men, admits to a bias in this matter. To Sol, one of the great injustices of the world is the fact that whales are on the endangered species list and dogs aren't.

This is not a weird attitude; an aversion to dogs has been a part of Jewish life for centuries.

In part, this cultural bias has to do with the fact that vicious dogs really were a danger in the *shtetl,* places that never heard of leash laws.

More to the point, there are passages in the Talmud that argue against "evil" or "bad" dogs—meaning dogs that bark too much, since it was supposed back then that the bark of a nasty dog could scare a person to death.

And Jewish tradition does not encourage the domestication of animals for frivolous purposes; God didn't put animals on this earth so you could have some overbred poodle named Princess yapping at your heels.

You want a good Jewish pet, bubbe? Try a goat; in Eastern Europe, it was common for Jewish families to keep goats in the house. As pets, goats are winners: they're friendly, they don't bark, and they're downright useful in homes without garbage disposals.

✳

Q *In the back of my favorite Jewish publication, there are always ads for* mohels. *Why do some of them have "Rev." before their names? Is there something about* mohels *they're not telling us?*

A This suspicious-sounding usage derives from the fact that there are lots of official jobs in Judaism—but only one generally accepted "title," that of rabbi.

So what's a cantor to do, or a *shochet* or a *mohel?* The handiest solution is the all-purpose title of reverend, a generic term for clergy of every stripe.

If seeing a "reverend" perform a *bris* still makes you suspicious, chew on this bit of historical trivia: the only Jewish chaplain during the Revolutionary War was referred to as "reverend" because he was not officially ordained as a rabbi. So was the first Jewish religious leader in historic Charleston, South Carolina.

And the "reverend" appellation doesn't mean that these guys are second-rate *mohels.* Every *mohel* is taught and certified by other *mohels,* who know their business. And that's a good thing, if you know what Sol means.

✳

Q *Sol, I enjoy going to synagogue, and I really respect the Jewish faith, but one thing really bothers me: why do Jews insist on naming every square inch of their synagogues, schools, and community centers after dead people? I mean, I sit in the Hyman Moscowitz pew in the Sophie Soapstein chapel; one of these days I expect to dry my hands from the Sammie Cohen memorial towel dispenser. Don't you think this is a trifle tacky?*

A First, get it out of your head that Jews are the only group to carry this naming business to extremes. Most religious groups, hard-pressed for funds, find memorialization an effective way to raise money.

But remember, too, that Judaism is a religion that goes to greater-than-average lengths to remember the dead. The mourners' *kaddish*, the observance of *Yahrtzeit*, these kinds of rituals tend to give the process of remembering departed relatives a greater importance in Jewish life.

So the memorial towel dispenser you mentioned might be

a comforting mechanism of remembrance for the bereaved family, as well as a good fund-raising gimmick. If you're lucky, somebody may name something bigger than a single floor tile after *you*.

As for tacky, Sol thinks the only really tacky part of this whole business is the fact that Jewish institutions are forced to rely on all kinds of fund-raising tricks because of skinflints who don't want to pay their way.

☀

Q *Sol, a lot of countries have chief rabbis. Israel even has several, one for the Sephardim and one for the Ashkenazim. Why don't we have one here in the United States, and if we did, would he be Orthodox, Conservative, or Reform?*

A A minor technicality called "separation of church and state" is why, bubbe.

Since there is no established state religion in the United States, and no religion that is even sanctioned in a semiofficial way—Arizona's efforts to establish Christianity as its official religion notwithstanding—it would be inappropriate for the government to designate a rabbinic spokesman for the Jewish population.

And the second part of your question points to the obvious impossibility of Jews themselves selecting a single spiritual leader. It strains credulity to imagine, say, Satmar Chasidim in Brooklyn accepting the spiritual authority of a Reconstructionist rabbi in California, whose idea of a *mikvah* is a redwood hot tub in the Hollywood Hills. It is equally implausible to imagine a caftaned Brooklynite rabbi winning the hearts of Reconstructionist Jews.

☀

Q *Why are so many doctors Jews? Please, do not give your typical quick-and-dirty answer. Give some thought to this one, Solly.*

A Are you suggesting that each and every one of Sol's answers does not require literally hours of meditation and study, not to mention consultation with the best authorities on this sad little planet? Sol would be insulted, except that he's too busy whipping out his hourly quota of 45 answers.

American Jews are clearly proud of the MDs in their midst; non-Jews, as in past eras, tend to stereotype Jewish doctors as somehow more talented in the arcane arts of medicine than their gentile colleagues.

Sol's own favorite doctor stereotype involves the funny vanity license plates these otherwise-humorless people tend to sport on their pricey cars, like "TUCHIS M.D.," and "C ME 2 P," apparently an example of what passes for humor among urologists.

Oh, yes, your question. Some observers have suggested that the Jewish interest in medicine has to do with the strong value placed on saving lives in Jewish law and tradition—the idea of *pikku'ah nefesh,* the fact that even important laws like the observance of the Sabbath can be set aside when it is a question of saving a life.

The status of doctors in the Jewish world wasn't exactly hurt by the fact that Maimonides, one of the real heavy-hitters of Jewish history, was a skilled physician in the last decades of the twelfth century.

So even in the dark recesses of our past, Jewish physicians were honored by the community, as well as their mothers, a fact that naturally spawned more of them.

Also, during the Middle Ages, there were all kinds of professions and occupations from which Jews were excluded; medicine provided a safe outlet for smart, talented Jews.

And because of the dispersion of the Jewish people from the Middle East, Jewish doctors helped spread medical knowledge from the great centers of learning around the Mediterranean. Jews may have been treated like dirt in Medieval Europe, but a number of royal families preferred Jewish doctors with their cutting-edge knowledge to the local chest-thumpers. Again, the high status of Jewish doctors made medicine an even more popular profession.

In modern America, too, bias played a role. Doctoring was one of the surest routes to success for young Jews back in the early decades of this century, when Jews were barred from many corporate boardrooms.

⁂

Q *Are there any Jewish jockeys? Is there any reason why Jews cannot become jockeys?*

A Sol has news for you: jockeys *ride* horses, they don't *eat* them. You obviously have never heard of Walter "Mousy" Blum, a prominent Jewish jockey in the 1960s, or Harry "Cocky" Feldman. You likewise appear ignorant of a family called the Rothschilds, who didn't race horses themselves, but owned about a million of them. And August Belmont, Sr., the Jewish tycoon who was a cofounder of the American Jockey Club.

Horse racing has never been a heavily Jewish sport—there aren't many of *those*, unless you count competitive shopping. But Jews have been represented at every level of the racing business, from owners and breeders to grooms and jockeys.

This isn't to say that it's been duck soup for Jews in the race game. Until the middle of this century, Jews were not widely accepted among the horsey set; Jews could own horses, but until the 1940s and 1950s, they were not generally admitted to the clubs that are the backbone of the racing world.

But it is also true that Jews may have a problem with a related aspect of horse racing—specifically, with gambling. Sol would never generalize about such complex matters, but in general, while Jewish authorities have not condemned the process of gambling, they have opposed professional or compulsive gambling.

So an occasional bet on some trotter will not get you in trouble, bubbe. But if you hang out at the track and squander all your hard-earned money on the ponies, you are violating the weight of Jewish tradition.

Q *In today's world, one sees very few prominent Jewish athletes. Have there ever been sports considered "Jewish," in the sense that Jews were present in more than a mere smattering?*

A You're right, Jews are real smatterers, doubtless because we are a mere smattering in the broader American population. This is a special problem in the area of athletics; people in our society live and die by their sports heroes, and in recent years, Jewish kids have had to stretch a little in looking for Jewish members of this elite fraternity.

If you're looking for sports *dominated* by Jews, try table tennis—at least in the old days, before the Chinese became such wizards at the sport and American Jews turned their athletic sights on exercise machines that simulate all kinds of sports without the fuss of actually participating in them.

In the 1920s and 1930s, many world champions in this glamorous sport were Jews, starting with Dr. Roland Jacobi. Sol has been unable to learn if Jacobi won great wealth endorsing high-tech table tennis paddles or after-shave lotions.

Or try boxing. In the 1920s, Jews dominated the fight game, with guys like Battling Levinsky, Benny Leonard, Louis "Kid" Kaplan, and Abe Goldstein pounding and battering their way to fame.

In this, Jewish boxers were not unlike their modern black counterparts; boxing was seen as a quick and dramatic way out of the ghetto.

Now, the only boxers being raised in Jewish homes have names like Rover and Rex.

Q *Dear Sol: Can Jews be optimists? I've been one all my life—a Jew, that is—and to be perfectly frank, we seem like a*

pretty gloomy lot. Is there something in the religion that keeps us from an optimistic viewpoint? In the culture?

A Sol would give you a snappy answer, but your letter made him too depressed.

As you might suspect, your question has enough nuances to keep a Talmudic scholar happy as a clam for about a lifetime. On second thought, scratch the clam, a food that would never pass the lips of our scholar.

As individuals, Jews are probably no more gloomy than anybody else in this crazy world, a place that sometimes makes optimism seem like a kind of mental illness.

Think about it: how would you judge the sanity of a person who remains optimistic in the face of the Greenhouse Effect, the collapse of world currencies, the proliferation of chemical weapons, and Donald Trump's divorce?

It may be that Jews, steeped in the idea of self-analysis that comes from both Judaism and psychiatry, think about the meaning of life in the face of these things, and so give the impression of gloominess.

On a cultural level, a lot of the historical threads that hold the Jewish community together are, at least on the surface, bummers.

So at weddings, the groom smashes a glass to make sure in the midst of all the festivities that we remember a more somber event—the destruction of the Temple. Jewish religious observance is full of reminders of the terrible moments in our collective history, moments as recent as the Second World War.

That being said, most rabbis insist that Judaism is inherently an optimistic religion. For every tragedy in Jewish history, there is a kind of miracle that follows. Unbearable slavery in Egypt was followed by the Exodus; the Holocaust was followed by the miraculous rebirth of Israel.

Messianism in its various forms adds to the sense of optimism many Jews feel. For the Reform, the idea of a Messiah has been transformed into an expectation of an earthly redemption for all people through the collective striving of men and women for goodness; for the Orthodox, the idea that the Messiah will come is a very real and positive element in their lives.

Sol is always impressed with the idea that Jewish optimism is a *pragmatic* optimism, based on gritty history, not fairy-tale dreams. Optimistic non-Jews tend to think that everything will work out fine; optimistic Jews suspect things will turn out poorly, but that something extraordinary will probably come from this always-lurking disaster.

Or, as Abraham Joshua Heschel once said, "I am an optimist against my better judgment."

Sol invites his loyal readers to contribute their own thoughts on Jewish optimism. Of course, he expects the worst.

☀

Q *Why are so many big New York camera and electronics stores run by Chasidic groups?*

A Your sensitive nose isn't sniffing out a *conspiracy*, is it?

As you suggest, many of the vast electronics and camera emporia in the Big Apple are owned and run by Chasidic families. Much of Sol's own computer equipment comes from a place affectionately known as "Kosher Kamera," which offers terrific prices, outstanding selections, and all the personality of a convention of undertakers.

This kind of enterprise has some unique advantages for tight-knit Orthodox groups. First, the rise of mail-order, high-tech operations made it possible for them to operate thriving businesses without leaving New York—and their *shuls,* kosher butchers, and those wonderful subways, which is how they get their relaxation.

Secondly, family-run establishments offered some very important advantages for observant Jews, including the ability to adjust their hours to allow for *davening* and study and to shut down for Jewish holidays and Shabbat.

And Chasids tend to have big families; owning your own labor-intensive retail business is a good way of making sure they're all gainfully employed in a safe, supportive environment.

Finally, these Chasidic guys were smart; they spotted high-tech gadgets as the coming thing, and they quickly took advantage of the boom.

The Unbearable Weirdness of Being

Strange Facts About Life at the End of the Twentieth Century

Q *Why do cellular telephone antennas have those little squiggles in them?*

A Cellular phones—Sol's wife persists in calling them "cellulite" phones, for reasons unknown in the realm of logic—operate by broadcasting your croaky little voice over the radio.

Now, radio transmission requires antennas of specific wavelengths. The correct wavelength for cellular phones would require an antenna several feet long.

But car phones were meant to appeal to the BMW-and-Volvo set, not truckers, to whom gigantic CB antennas are a source of perverse pride.

So the antennas were shortened by means of those little squiggles. In an electronic sense, the antennas are long and tacky; physically, they're short, classy little numbers. Get it?

Q *When did they start fluoridating water in this country, and is it really a Communist plot? And do Orthodox Jews have any qualms about drinking water with additives like fluoride?*

A Where have you been for the past 30 years, under a rock? Conspiracy buffs in the sophisticated 1990s worry about supermarket scanners and the Common Market, not fluoride.

The beneficial affects of fluoride compounds on the choppers was first noted in the early 1800s in Europe, when dentists observed that people whose water supplies naturally contained high concentrations of fluoride had pearly whites that never needed the dentist's drill—a good thing, considering the crude dental equipment available in those days.

By the middle of the last century, fluoride was available as a patent medicine in various parts of the world, along with Aunt Wanda's Wonder Juice, which cured constipation and brain fog.

In the 1940s, several communities began adding fluoride to their water supplies, led by Grand Rapids, Michigan, Newburgh, New York, and Brantford, Ontario.

This bold policy immediately generated outcries from some religious folks who were opposed to what they saw as "compulsory medication," not to mention crackpots concerned about Communist plots to poison the children of America.

As it turned out, if the Communists *had* been looking around for ways to subvert America, they'd have done a lot better by getting into the DDT business, or becoming network television executives.

And don't worry about the halachic implications of fluoride. Since it is not ingested as a food—and since it is not derived from any prohibited food products—it's perfectly okay. Your teeth will thank you.

Q *In the 1960s, why did hijackers always want to go to Cuba?*

A 'Cause Cuba was close and didn't extradite, is why. And generally, hijackers were dumb enough to think Fidel was a kind of fuzzy teddy bear.

The latter turned out to be an unfortunate miscalculation; most participants in the hijacking boom, which peaked in 1969 when hijacking was so common that airliners on the East Coast all carried approach maps for Havana Airport, ended up in the slammer—and Fidel ended up with whatever loot they managed to acquire.

In that landmark year, there were some 71 hijackings in this country—and 58 of them went to Havana.

There is also the imitation factor. Let's be honest: guys who hijack airplanes aren't exactly rocket scientists. So the early hijackings provided a model that made the decision easy for many of these clowns, who followed the yellow brick road straight into Fidel's prisons.

⚶

Q *Why do they always hang the tag from the toe of a corpse in the morgue and not from the neck or wrist or somewhere else?*

A Excuse Sol for saying so, but there's nothing wrong with your question that a little reasoning wouldn't cure.

Think about it: morgues house their reluctant guests in air-conditioned comfort, in little refrigerated cases in which the departed recline on sliding trays. Not exactly your basic Barcalounger, no siree.

Tags on toes, therefore, make sense from a practical point of view; they provide identification information in an accessible location, and they're attached to a part of the body that's easy to find and easy to hook things to.

On a more personal note, Sol respectfully urges you to focus on cheerier things, like nuclear waste and the national debt.

Q *How come when I need to change my subscription on my magazines I end up sending the change of address form to some place in Colorado? Is there a great big printing press out there where national magazines line up for time on the press and on the mailroom schedule? What gives?*

A In this wonderfully technological age, electronic communication makes all manner of wonders accessible even to the publishers of the kind of shlock you probably read.

So the printing press can be in one city, the editorial offices in another—and something called a "fulfillment" house, a wonderfully ambiguous term if Sol ever heard one, is usually in some forsaken but central part of the country. Some place like Colorado Springs, Colorado, or Marion, Ohio.

What fulfillment houses do is keep track of your subscriptions, dun you when you fall behind, and send you those incredible renewal notices about a month after your year's subscription starts, something in the industry they call "renewal at birth." Sol finds this process almost as annoying as those little "blow in" cards that spew out of most major publications and leave a trail of litter.

Q *Sol, I keep seeing these pink ribbons tied to car radio antennas, and I'm wondering: is this some sort of strange code for single people? Pleas for hostages in some distant land? Inform us, Sol.*

A Sol *could* give you the quick-and-dirty answer, but your question presents a rare opportunity to shed light into the finely tuned mechanisms of the Answer Man business. Pay attention, now.

Sol began by asking two cop friends about those pink ribbons. The responses from the boys in blue were as follows: "I dunno." And "What ribbons?"

Undaunted, Sol ran a sophisticated computer search on the

topic. The only thing that turned up was something about the daring use of ribbons in last season's Paris fashions.

Frustrated, Sol spewed venom at an editor friend of his about the low quality of the questions sent by readers.

"Oh, the pink ribbons?" she said instantly. "That's Mothers Against Drunk Driving." No doubt this editor covets the prestige and pay of the Answer Man position, and thus spent many hours in research.

Nevertheless, the answer was a correct one; the pink ribbons, displayed on so many car antennas these days, are part of a yearly promotional effort by Mothers Against Drunk Driving. Every winter holiday season, the group distributes millions of ribbons—some 1.5 million in Maryland alone—to remind drivers not to drink and drive.

Q *Put on your geographer's hat, Sol. Why are state lines in the Western states straight and neat, while the Eastern states look like they were surveyed by someone who had been drinking?*

A You have to understand, the guys who laid out the Western states had a problem: most of them had never been west of the Appalachians. Worse, the information they were working from was as thin as the hair on Sol's head.

So the combination of plenty of land to go around, and not too many people who knew what was where, led the surveyors to plot many state lines according to criteria that didn't require first-hand observation—namely, latitude and longitude lines.

In the East, of course, it was different; boundaries were literally staked out by the people who lived there. Natural features like rivers, mountain ranges, and the like provided convenient, if serpentine, dividing points, and helped resolve conflicts over neighboring claims.

Actually, if the government had accepted Thomas Jefferson's scheme for laying out states, the West would be neatly

laid out in precise rectangles, with names like Polypotamia, Metropotamia, and the like, according to the historian Daniel Boorstin in his trilogy, *The Americans*.

Q *Tell me about the flag of Libya. In pictures I've seen, it just looks like a blue piece of cloth.*

A Muammar Qaddafi may be Mister Excitement, but the Libyan flag is strictly dullsville. It is, as you suggest, a simple rectangle of greenish-blue cloth, about as inspirational as a shower curtain.

A few years back, when Libya had better relations with its fellow Arab states, its flag sported a flashier design of red, white, and blue bands, with an eagle in the center—identical to the flags used by Egypt and Syria, a reflection of the planned confederation of those countries.

But relations deteriorated after the Camp David accords in 1978. Syria, in a bold stroke of international relations, substituted a couple of stars for the eagle. And Libya went to the plain piece of cloth—nothing to get excited about, but a heck of a lot easier for Libya's would-be Betsy Rosses.

Q *Why do pens in banks always run out of ink?*
A Okay, let's take this real slow. Let's say you're a real macher and you own a bank. People are coming in all day long using your pens to write checks and things. Some of them forget to put them back in the little holders, so the points are exposed to all that dry bank air; some gonifs swipe them, despite the chains, cables, and booby traps you use to prevent thievery. Angry people write hard enough to make 35 copies—without carbon paper.

So what are you going to use at the counter, your Mont Blanc with the 14-carat tip? Your gold bar mitzvah Cross?

Not if you're a macher; you use the cheapest, most easily replaceable pen on the face of the earth. You buy refills by the truckload.

And that's an answer you can take all the way to the bank.

Q *Is "Muzak" really supposed to alter our moods? Is it true that they use it at the Pentagon, and if so, what for?*
A Muzak, which is a trade name for a specific brand of piped-in music, does indeed try to tickle your neurons. It is based on the concept of "stimulus progression," which—according to Muzak gurus—means that 15-minute chunks of music can be programmed to provide a calculated psychological lift for your average numbed-out office drone like Sol.

Muzak officials take pains to distinguish their product from generic "elevator music," which apparently calms people by boring them to death.

And yes, indeed, the Pentagon has in the past used Muzak in its war against snooping. The idea is that Muzak in top-secret corridors will mask sensitive conversations. So generals and their ilk can feel secure talking about how to overthrow governments and receive payoffs from defense contractors and other favorite Pentagon topics.

Q *Who invented popcorn? And is there a real Orville Redenbacher, or is this the same kind of fakeout as Betty Crocker and Ann Page?*

A Popcorn is as old as the hills, so to speak—it predates microwave ovens, even. The American Indians reportedly invented the art of roasting whole ears of corn over open fires until some of the kernels popped, and others burned to cinders. Presumably, the Indians mostly ate the popped ones. But Sol's kid sister always loved the charred, unpopped kernels, so maybe some Indians did, too.

When Sol was a mere lad, he used to be fascinated by "The Electric Theater" at a museum in Chicago, where an entire ear of corn was strapped into a kind of electric chair for vegetables, and zapped until popcorn sprayed all over the

auditorium. Sol does not recommend this technique for household use.

And yes, Orville Redenbacher is a real character, an agronomist who developed new, more poppable varieties of corn to feed a world with a collective case of the munchies. Redenbacher's company is truly a family business—part of what was once the Beatrice Foods mega-company. So much for Orville's down-home image.

✳

Q *When and why were the words "under God" added to the Pledge of Allegiance?*

A Sol remembers that event well: it was 1954, and Sol had just learned the darned Pledge. Then Congress had to go and change it . . .

The "under God" line was added in response to pressure from church and patriotic groups—and as a concession to the McCarthyism rampant in those days. Some people saw the insertion of "under God" as a powerful blow against the godless Reds, who would now know better than to mess with the good old U.S. of A.

This despite the fact that nine out of ten school children fervently believe that one word in the pledge is "forwhichit." So much for stirring messages.

So popular was the idea of inserting these words that Capitol Hill was literally flooded with mail in favor of the 15 or so bills adding one variety or another of the "under God" phrasing. The bill that ultimately passed was authored by two Republicans from Michigan—Senator Homer Ferguson and Representative Louis Rabaut.

Interestingly, school children invariably believe that the Pledge dates back to Revolutionary War days. Not true; in fact, the Pledge of Allegiance made its first appearance in 1892. The authorship of the Pledge has always been in doubt; the Library of Congress, as close to a final authority as you can get for these kinds of questions, attributes it to Frances

Bellamy, an editor of *The Youth's Companion,* the magazine that first published it.

Q *Why are the buttons on men's and women's shirts on different sides?*
A This falls into the category of the "Eternal Mysteries of Life." In other words, there are lots of theories, very few facts.

Buttons have been around since the days of the ancient Egyptians, but it took several thousand years for folks to figure out that they were useful for holding shirts together.

Differences between men's and women's shirts—aside from their contents—showed up as early as the sixteenth century; some historians have actually studied old portraits to check out the buttons, which gives you an idea of the deep thinking required in that profession.

One popular theory about the gender difference in shirts goes like this: back in the Middle Ages, men tended to dress themselves, while women who really counted—princesses and that sort of thing—had servants to do the job.

Most people are right-handed. So, the theory goes, men's shirts were designed for right-handed self-buttoners, while the ladies' shirts were designed from the perspective of servants. In other words, if you were a right-handed woman of ordinary parentage, you were out of luck. This may explain why progress in civilization has been so slow.

Q *I keep seeing ads for these places that promise you can make money at home addressing envelopes. Is this a good business?*
A Sure it's a good business—for the gonif who places the ad. In case you haven't noticed, this is the computer age; even Sol's Stone Age computer can address about a billion envelopes in an hour or so without the assistance of unemployed housewives and college students.

So what do you get when you send in your 20 bucks? A good job and a business that's going to make you the Donald Trump of the envelope-addressing industry?

Not a chance. Chances are, what you'll get is advice about how you can play the suckers yourself—by placing your very own ad (which, naturally, involves mailing something in an envelope you have addressed), and then raking in the bucks from those poor shlemiels who don't realize that this gimmick has been around since early man slithered out of the slime— and then immediately began to look for ways to get back in.

米

Q *On TV advertisements, why do they always tell people to call a toll-free number "except in Nebraska"? What's wrong with Nebraska, anyway?*

A Are you suggesting something might be wrong with a state sometimes called "the Gateway to Iowa"? Shame on you, bubbe.

My late grandmother had a standard response to questions of this sort: "What, you can't see what's right in front of your nose?" This generally meant that she didn't know, either.

Nebraska has become the mail-order Capital of the Universe because of its fortunate geography. Coast-to-coast advertisers for low-cost life insurance, "reducing aids," and gadgets that slice, dice, and otherwise mangle your food can save a bundle on long-distance phone service by being right in the center of things. It also doesn't hurt that the overhead costs—labor, buildings, and that sort of thing—are lower in the middle of nowhere.

Answering services for electronic shlock houses aren't the only ones who have learned this shrewd trick. When you dial an 800 airline number, or the reservation number for a major hotel chain or car rental firm, chances are you're talking to a genuine Nebraskan.

Why the "except in Nebraska" warning? Because advertisers pay more for 800 service that allows both in-state and out-of-state calls. That's another advantage of Nebraska; the state's tiny population means that the fewest number of potential customers will be turned off by having to dial a separate non-800 number.

Q *Sol, how is money laundered? Does it take any special equipment, or is it a purely financial transaction?*

A Sheesh, don't you know bubkes? Dirty money needs to be cleaned up, but you won't find any detergents that can do the job.

Money laundering is the shady practice of taking ill-gotten gains, and processing them through legitimate businesses so that you can buy your moll tawdry jewels and things.

Let's say you make a killing in the illicit cheese blintz market. You can't just take your dough and put it in the corner bank, not without various federal authorities breathing

down your scruffy little neck. Banks in this country are obligated to report large cash transactions to the feds.

So you stash your money in an offshore bank and rake in the interest. Or you buy a casino or a big restaurant, which deals heavily in cash, and you mix your ill-gotten gains in with the take from the salad bar, a technique that gave Las Vegas a lot of its glitter.

Human creativity being what it is, there are an infinite number of ways to launder money. As they say, it all comes out in the wash.

***

Q *How did mah-jongg make its way from China to an English gambling game to my friend Rose's Coral Gables home?*

A The way you put it, it sounds almost like a conspiracy from the Dark East. Sol likes it.

It's a little shocking to remember that in the early 1920s, mah-jongg was a major craze with the American middle class—and therefore with the American Jewish community. Today, of course, we've outgrown such nonsense; we play Pictionary and talk about dishes made with sun-dried tomatoes. The march of culture, and so on.

But to answer your question: mah-jongg probably does trace back to China, in some form or another. It was popularized by Joseph P. Babcock, who took the basic Chinese game, invented modern terminology, and patented the whole shmeer. In fact, the mah-jongg craze in the 1920s may have been the first nationwide fad created by sophisticated marketers using techniques that would someday give us Hula Hoops and Pet Rocks.

Mah-jongg is a four-handed game similar to rummy; you accumulate sets, using 152 little tiles with ivory faces. A truly trivial pursuit, if you get Sol's meaning.

***

Q *Recently, when I was in a department store, I noticed those little bumps on the shiny surface between the "up" and the "down" escalators. Are those bumps for what I think they're for? Are department stores really concerned that grown adults will use the place between escalators as slides?*

A One can never be too conservative in estimating the maturity and good sense of your average American citizen, especially in this age of liability overkill.

So indeed, those little bumps are subtle reminders to hurried shoppers that the obvious shortcut—swift though the descent might be—would also have a pretty unpleasant impact on a certain part of the anatomy, namely the tuchis.

Q *Why do librarians always hush people up in the library, but when they talk on the phone or to each other, they speak in normal voices? I think this is very unfair.*

A To be fair to librarians, one reason they speak in normal voices is the fact that it's very difficult to whisper on the telephone. This wouldn't be a problem if public libraries were as prosperous as, say, Exxon; then, they could afford to hire some people to answer the phones, some to talk to patrons, and some to sit out in front and keep a sharp eye on characters like you.

But librarians work for some of the biggest cheapskates in the world—the American public. So have pity on the poor souls, why don'tcha.

Q *Why do they have signs saying "check your gas"—halfway down the ramps to some expressways? What do they think you're going to do, back up if your tank is too low?*

A Sol just adores these highway questions, which open up for our perusal the vast landscape of human illogic.

There actually is a queer sort of rationality to these signs. Thousands of deep-thinking citizens every year hop on the

local expressway and promptly run out of gas—costing the state a hefty chunk of change in emergency road services, not to mention the hazards posed by dead cars.

As for backing up on the ramps, this is strongly discouraged; the idea is for the signs to remind you to look at that nasty "E" on your fuel gauge, and, if necessary, get off at the very next exit.

Q *What does a minister without portfolio do? Why doesn't he or she have a portfolio? What does he or she have to do to get one? What is inside the portfolio? Is it real leather, or tacky vinyl?*

A From your letter, Sol can tell that you are a person of intellect and education, given to solving the great puzzles of our age. With people like you, we need not worry about the future of Western civilization.

"Portfolio," in this context, refers to the "office and functions of a minister of state or member of a cabinet," according to Webster. It has nothing to do with the little satchel that Ariel Sharon once used to shlep around his Publishers Clearing House sweepstakes entry form back in the days when he was a minister without portfolio.

In Israel, as in other countries, a minister without portfolio is a cabinet-level official not assigned a specific ministry—all the perks of power, but none of the hassle. Not a bad job, if you can manage it.

Q *What are those red balls I've seen strung on electrical wires that hang over highways in some parts of the country? Some kind of radar?*

A *Radar?* Are you one of those shnooks who think people are always observing them on hidden cameras?

If you look closely, you'll see that these balls on the power lines tend to be around hospitals and airfields. Hospitals these days generally have helipads for med-evac choppers; airfields have . . . well, airplanes and helicopters.

It doesn't take much of a stretch of the gray matter to draw a conclusion; these orange or red gizmos are designed to keep helicopters and other low-flying aircraft from plowing into the power lines with catastrophic results.

Q *Why are Florida drivers so bad? I thought it might have something to do with all the retired New York cab drivers living in the state.*

A Once, Sol ignorantly believed that this generalization about Florida drivers was pure prejudice.

But then he visited an elderly relative living in St. Pete, a man to whom stoplights were purely ornamental. And Sol became a believer.

The statistics, alas, do not fully back up this impression. According to a spokesman for the American Automobile Association, the standard measure for a state's auto-accident rate is the number of traffic deaths per 100,000 vehicle miles.

By that standard, Florida is a dangerous place, but not quite as dangerous as Mississippi and New Mexico.

The national average was 2.6 deaths per 100,000 vehicle miles. Florida turned in a scary 3.2 score; New Mexico led the list at 4.1. When you consider that there's hardly any traffic in that state, that number is truly scary.

The safest state for driving? Minnesota, with a minuscule rate of 1.6.

But there's another possibility here: the *accident* rate in Florida could be high, but the *death* rate low—because half the drivers there never go faster than 10 miles per hour, even on the expressways.

But Sol was unable to back up this theory with hard statistics, so for now, you'll have to go with the AAA figures.

Q *Why do big UPS trucks have those little brushes over the wheels? I haven't seen them on other 18-wheelers. Does this have something to do with the fact that UPS delivers my packages so much faster than the postal service?*

A Sol doesn't know if the brush-like devices actually speed delivery, but they sure as heck benefit drivers sharing the highways with the ever-present brown behemoths.

According to a UPS spokesman, these gadgets are "splash and spray devices." They may have good inventors over at UPS, but when it comes to naming their products, they leave something to be desired.

Anyway, these devices cut down substantially on spray coming up the wheel well and on "side spray"—that blast of water you can get when being passed by one of these big trucks on a rainy day.

The reason you don't see them on other trucks is that the devices were designed by the folks at UPS, and are manufactured specifically for the big shipping firm.

Q *Why do Arab groups plaster the walls in so many big American cities with posters in Arabic? I can't imagine that this is a very effective form of advertising, since most folks in this country don't read this language.*

A Sol submitted your question to several so-called experts, who came back with answers every bit as implausible as the posters themselves.

When experts disagree, Sol generally turns to that last resort of Answer Men, logic.

First, it's the impression that counts in political rhetoric, not the words. When it enters your congested brain pan that *every single stoplight signal box in Chicago* has a poster in Arabic, it sort of hits home, and you begin looking over your shoulder, as if these people were absolutely everywhere.

This is not exactly a bad way for a small minority to make its presence felt.

There's a second theory that has some plausibility. Arab populations in American cities tend to be fairly dispersed and, because of the relatively small size of this community, they tend to lack established organs of communication, like newspapers and radio programs. So the posters serve an informative purpose.

⌖

Q *Sol, this is really getting to me. At my local grocery store—part of a big chain—they have all these idiotic gimmicks. One week it's "Hawaii week," and the checkers are all dressed in flowered shirts; the next, it's "blue jeans week," and they're decked out in blue jeans and Western shirts. Is this supposed to make me want to buy more frozen bagels or something? How stupid do these people think we are?*

A Not stupid, bubbe, just gullible, a judgment unfortunately confirmed by the fact that these sales gimmicks almost always produce gains at the cash registers.

One key idea behind these promotions was actually discovered decades ago, when the Western Electric company

commissioned a study in one of its manufacturing plants. First, they found that positive changes in the workplace improved worker morale and productivity. Then, they started taking away those changes—and lo and behold, even *negative* changes boosted worker output.

The same holds true for marketing; we poor shmendricks out there in Consumerland seem to respond positively to even silly changes in the places where we so readily drop our hard-earned money.

Of course, we'd probably respond even more to price cuts. But if corporate planners have to choose between decreased profits and blue jeans for checkers, you can guess which one they'll choose.

FIVE

☀

Yiddish, English, and Other Exotic Languages

Q *Solly, I wanted to ask you about the difference between dreck and shlock, two subjects about which I thought you would have a certain expertise. Are they synonymous?*

A One of the qualities of greatness in the Answer Man business is the ability to never allow one's personal feelings to cause gridlock on the great Highway of Knowledge.

So let us proceed, and you'll hear from Sol's attorney in the morning.

Strictly speaking, the two Yiddish words mean almost the same thing—junk, trash, the kind of thing you might buy on sale—at a place with flashing lights and salesmen in checked polyester suits.

In common usage, "dreck" is used to refer more to creative products—movies, books, and yes, even newspaper columns. "Shlock," on the other hand, usually refers to lousy merchandise, things that you'd be likely to buy at the "shlock houses" that keep Sol garbed in the latest fashions.

Of the two, "dreck" is the stronger term; some people still think it's a term you would not use in mixed company. In today's verbal climate, of course, "dreck" sounds as innocent as "marshmallow."

Q *I was thinking about buying some gold bullion, and I got to wondering: why does the word "bullion" apply both to gold bricks and soup?*

A There's nothing wrong with you that a good dictionary wouldn't cure, bubbe. In fact, you're confusing two different words: "bouillon," which is the broth you sip when you're sick, and "bullion," referring to uncoined gold or silver. Fort Knox is not the nation's primary depository for beef soup.

Q *I was in Florida recently, and naturally, the word "kitsch" came to mind. Seriously, now, what does it mean, and where does it come from? It sounds Yiddish.*

A Kitsch probably comes from your living room, but that's another story. As a term used by the artsy set, it means a work executed with a degree of skill, but not even a faint whiff of taste. Lava lamps are kitschy; paintings of German shepherds rendered on black velvet are kitschy in the extreme.

The origins of the word are unclear; the late John Ciardi, once the nation's unofficial arbiter of language, guessed that it's a Yiddish corruption of a similar German word, which means roughly what it means in today's usage.

Q *My Dad had some medical tests recently, and when I asked him how it went, he sighed and said: "They gave me*

the whole Megillah. *I've heard the expression a million times, but I don't really know its origin. What gives?*

A As you no doubt surmised, the *Megillah* has two layers of meaning. The first and most important is its religious meaning; *Megillah* is a Hebrew word meaning "scroll." In common usage, the word is used to refer to the Book of Esther in the Bible.

But language is a wonderfully democratic process; no matter what the "authorities" say, whether they be linguistic or religious, evocative common usages tend to spread far and wide.

So it was with *Megillah*. The Book of Esther is not known for its brevity. So over the years, "the whole *Megillah*" became a way of referring to anything unusually lengthy and thorough.

Q *When I was young, my mother used to harass me about buttoning my blouses right up to my chin. What she'd say was, "I can see right down to your* pupik." *I never really understood what a* pupik *was, but I suspected it was a little off-color; every time she'd say it in front of friends, I was*

mortified. Now that I'm an adult, I think I can stand it: what is a pupik, *Sol?*

A If your *pupik*'s off-color, it's just because you haven't taken a bath in about a month.

Technically speaking, a *pupik* is just a belly button. Suggesting that your shirt was open down to your *pupik* was a typical instance of parental hyperbole.

And *pupik* has a wonderfully raunchy sound to it that makes it seem more risque than it actually is.

⋇

Q *Every day on the business news they talk about "pork belly futures." Now I don't want to sound ignorant, Sol, but what are pork bellies, and why would anyone want to buy them?*

A Your question points to one of the truly fascinating aspects of life in this age of information overload—the day we can hear an idea or phrase almost every day without having even the faintest idea of its meaning.

In pursuing the answer to your question, Sol even encountered a commodities trader who has actually dealt in pork bellies, and who could provide only an embarrassed shrug when asked just what it was he traded.

Pork bellies are standardized chunks of butchered hogs that provide a convenient way for the people who deal in these things to do their business.

Sol checked out the official rules of the Chicago Mercantile Exchange—a shocking document in itself, since it is commonly assumed that commodities traders would not recognize a rule if they tripped over one.

Anyway, the rules define pork bellies as the cleaned abdomens of sows—obviously with the organs, bone, and cartilage trimmed away, along with most of the abdominal surface fat.

To use the Exchange's raucously humorous language, they are "green, square-cut, clear, seedless bellies from a federally inspected packing plant." Sol might think of tossing his cookies, if he could figure out just what the heck these guys are talking about.

A certified pork belly also has to be free from bruises, cuts, or signs of putrefaction, a fact that will no doubt reassure non-kosher consumers. The things are frozen and then traded in units of about 38,000.

Of course, a Jew on the commodities exchange might do better to trade gefilte fish futures.

Q *Sol, what is a tycoon? You hear the word all the time, and it just occurred to me that I don't have the foggiest idea what it actually* means. *Obviously, Donald Trump is a tycoon and I am not. What is the difference?*

A You mean besides brains, wealth, and a boat about the size of Rhode Island? Not much.

Originally, "tycoon" meant what Donnie Trump would probably like to be some day—a great prince, a member of the nobility. It derives from the Japanese *taikun,* or shogun.

Later—probably in nineteenth-century America—the term was applied to great men of commerce and industry. It was an admiring term, in those days of innocence. Today, we'd be more likely to use a word like "gonif" to refer to these guys, but that's another program.

Q *Okay, Sol, I've been reading about this business with the Polish primate, Cardinal Glemp, and I was baffled by this question: what in tarnation is a "primate"? I always thought it was a kind of monkey. But this guy's a bishop, I'm sure he doesn't even believe in evolution. Can you shed some light on this mystery?*

A Ha, every reader thinks he's a comedian. You guys have no *idea* how much raw talent it takes to be funny.

"Primate" is, in fact, a gloriously versatile word. In its raw meaning, it refers to the Big Blintz—the first in rank in some hierarchy. So the chief bishop of Poland is the primate, because he's the top Catholic in the land.

But we've also come to refer to the class of mammals—including ordinary Americans, as well as chimpanzees and the like—as "primates," because technically, at least, we represent the very pinnacle of the animal kingdom.

This, of course, is a matter of some debate, especially in light of this year's television lineup and Miller Lite commercials.

☀

Q *Recently, somebody asked me how I felt "in my* kishkas." *I didn't let on that I didn't know what he meant, but I had this vague sense that he was saying something distasteful. Is this something you can refer to in polite company?*

A Who do you think Sol is, Miss Manners? Give the Answer Man a break.

To be honest, Sol has always found the entire matter of *kishkas* to be somewhat distasteful. From a technical point of view, after all, *kishkas* refer to the intestines. And *kishka* denotes that so-called delicacy in which meat is stuffed into an intestine casing and served to disbelieving diners at bar mitzvah parties throughout the land.

Kishka in Jewish cuisine is not unlike the similarly named and equally hideous dish that Poles eat, and which moved one polka writer to pen the immortal song, "Who Stole the *Kishka?*," which is to Polish celebrations what "Hava Nagila" is to Jewish *simchas*.

In the context to which you refer, "in the *kishkas*" means something like "in your guts." Not exactly elegant speech, but gets the idea across. When some inarticulate person asks you how you feel "in your *kishkas*," he's asking how you really feel, on a gut, emotional level.

Q *Dear Sol: My Aunt Rose spent the past 50 years as a milliner, which means, in case you're interested, that she made hats. But where did the word come from? Is it Yiddish?*

A If Sol were you, he'd let old Aunt Rose retire. It's not to your credit that you work your elderly relatives to the bone.

As for your question, milliners are called milliners because once upon a time, especially fine hats were made in—you guessed it—Milan. In case your geography is weak, Milan is in Italy.

It's true that many milliners in the early days of this century were Jews from the Old Country. But the term is as Yiddish in origin as "ravioli."

Q *Sol, I read a lot of newspapers, and I keep thinking about those "weasel words" we hear from the lips of our*

*leaders. Do weasels really speak this way? Isn't that a slander
on the animal kingdom?*

A It's not nice to steal lines from Sol, you gonif. Although
the origins of the term are somewhat unclear, we do know
that the phrase was popularized by Teddy Roosevelt, who in
1916 criticized his own bureaucracy with this immortal
phrase: "When a weasel sucks eggs, the meat is sucked out of
the egg. If you use a weasel word after another, there is
nothing left of the other."

In other words, weasel words are words without content,
the kind of thing you get in White House news conferences.

Animal protection advocates might well consider the political use of this term a slur against a perfectly respectable
member of the animal kingdom, but that's the word business
for you; it's a jungle out there, bubbe.

Q *When does something become trivia? Is it like antiques, where a certain number of years must pass before something is considered trivia?*

A "Trivia" is one of those wonderfully elastic words in our language whose meanings depend entirely on who's doing the talking, or trivializing.

Strictly speaking, trivia refers to something that's trivial—something so unimportant that no person with more than half a brain would take an interest in it.

But with the proliferation of games and contests designed to test our knowledge of boring facts, the word has taken on a more positive meaning, having to do with highly cherished but thoroughly insignificant nuggets of information. The name of Abe Lincoln's secretary of war is a matter of "history"; the name of his pet hamster is "trivia."

To answer your question directly: something becomes trivia when knowing about it makes you popular at parties, or wins you free prizes from radio stations. The passage of time has nothing to do with it.

⌇

Q *Why is a cul-de-sac always described as quiet, and how much less would a realtor get if a house on a cul-de-sac was described as a house on a dead end?*

A You've put your finger on an important element of salesmanship—the ability to define the terminology.

In the case of cul-de-sac, the word derives from the French term meaning something like "the bottom of the bag." Or, worse, a "blind diverticulum or pouch," as Webster's so indelicately puts it. Pass Sol the airsickness bag, please.

Needless to say, a "cul-de-sac home" would have very little cachet if homebuyers understood a lick of French. But long ago, marketers learned that anything said in French conveys an aura of class, and that it matters not a whit what the word or phrase actually means.

So "cul-de-sac" came to mean a street without an outlet,

or, more specifically, a dead end in a classy part of town. The automatic use of the adjective "quiet" was just one more refinement of the marketers' dark arts.

While we're on the subject, Sol has always found it interesting how certain words become attached to other words and phrases—like "quiet" to cul-de-sac, or "packing" to hurricane-force winds, as in "Hurricane Moshe, packing 70-mile-an-hour winds, is threatening the Gulf coast. . . ." Hurricanes never have 70-mile-an-hour winds, or feature 70-mile-an-hour winds; just *pack*. Curious, *nu?*

Q *Where did we get the word "seersucker," and what did it mean?*

A Seersucker is a corruption of a Persian term—*shir-o-shakar,* which means something along the lines of "milk and sugar."

Somewhere along the line, the term came to apply to a thin linen fabric made in India, with a crepe-like surface and a striped pattern that some people have described as less than classy.

Once, imported fabrics had a certain cachet to them; now, of course, you can go to any discount emporium and load up on clothes made in faraway places with strange-sounding names. And the Persian connection is lost in the mists of history; it's difficult envisioning any of the current crop of ayatollahs dressed in snappy seersucker suits while berating their numerous enemies.

Q *People talk about being hoisted on their own petards, and I must confess, I'm not sure if I have a petard or not. Is this something it's safe to talk about in mixed company?*

A Well, that depends. Technically, at least, there's nothing unseemly about your or anybody else's petard.

In fact, the word in question refers to a small device used

by primitive armies to blow holes in fortress doors. According to the folks at Oxford University Press, who collect such arcane facts for their *Oxford English Dictionary*, a soldier who wielded such a weapon was called a "petardeer."

We owe the common expression "hoisted on one's petard" to Will Shakespeare, who apparently thought he was being cute when he wrote in *Hamlet:* "For 'tis the sport to have the engineer/Hoist with his own petard." Presumably the Bard was referring to the process of skewering oneself with one's own trickery—although Sol must add, in the interests of accuracy, that there's another meaning having to do more with intestinal gas than with weaponry. But this *is* a family publication.

Q *Sol, why can't Jews agree about how to spell such common words as "Chasid"? Pardon my spelling.*

A Sol has news for you bubbe; Jews don't have the slightest problem spelling these words in Yiddish and Hebrew, from whence they spring. In case you haven't noticed, these languages use different alphabets than English; there is not a one-to-one correspondence between the two alphabets, so transliteration is sometimes a hit-or-miss affair.

Here, Sol will defer to Leo Rosten, who has done more than anybody to explain Yiddish to the masses.

According to Rosten, there have been numerous attempts to create a standard system for the transliteration of Yiddish into English, all of which have crashed against the stubborn strength of tradition, regional variation, and plain old bullheadedness. Even the American Jewish Press Association, which—as you might imagine—gets a lot of headaches over this spelling stuff, has laid out some basic standards. As you noticed, few of them are actually observed.

But if it bothers you, think about poor Muammar Qaddafi. Or is it Qaddhafi, or Gaddafi, or Gadaffi? Apparently there are several dozen spellings of the fellow's name. No wonder he acts confused about his place in the world.

Q *Sol, what's the difference between a temple, a syna-gogue, and a shul?*

A Not an easy question; like so many things in life, the "shul/synagogue/temple" debate depends on who's doing the talking. To some Orthodox folks, a shul is a place for *serious* worship, while a temple is a big building with an organ. To more Reform-minded Jews, shul evokes images from Chaim Potok novels: bare light bulbs dangling from the ceiling, musty old volumes of Talmud, no air conditioning.

The problem is that most people in the United States speak English—and exact translations from the myriad traditions out of which Jews spring are hard to come by.

In a nutshell, the answer to your question is as follows: "synagogue" is a Middle English or Latin word that specifi-cally refers to the regular assembly of people for purposes of worship; technically, a synagogue is a bunch of people, not a building.

This is an important point. The word "temple," with a lowercase "t," refers to a specific place, a building—just as "Temple" refers to the Great Temple of Jerusalem. On the other hand, "synagogue" implies portability. You can have a synagogue wherever there are Jews, a great advantage after the destruction of the Temple.

And "shul," which derives from the Greek *schola,* places an added emphasis on the idea of learning, as well as worship.

Q *Where does the word "cantor" come from? It sounds suspiciously like some Christian musical terms, like "cantata."*

A The crafty old English language can't slip one past *you.* "Cantor" is derived from the Latin, and means—literally—a singer. Somewhere in the 1500s, it began to be associated with a singer of liturgical music, or the leader of a choir.

Curiously, "cant" in the old days meant "to sing"—or "to

whine," an allusion that some cantors might find offensive.

In Hebrew, of course, these soaring-voiced folks are called *hazzan* or *sh'liah tzibbur,* which means "emissaries of the congregation."

❋

Q *Who was John Doe, and why has he been immortalized in our language as a person with no name?*

A What'd you want, Yakov Rabinowitz?

In point of fact, John Doe as a name for unknown persons derives from eighteenth-century England. Various authorities have questioned the precise derivation of the term; generally, they agree that Mr. Doe was born because his name sounds like it should be a common one—even though it isn't.

The term also had a legal connotation; in discussions of hypothetical trials, John Doe was generally the plaintiff, Richard Roe the defendant. Richard Roe died somewhere along the line.

❋

Q *The expression "a fly in the ointment"—is this from the Talmud?*

A Close but no cigar. Try Ecclesiastes 10:1: "dead flies make the ointment of the perfumer fetid and putrid; so doth a little folly outweigh wisdom and honour." A graphic allusion, but you have to admit: it gets the idea across.

❋

Q *Why is some silver "sterling"?*

A Sterling refers to the English silver penny that had its origins in Norman times. Generally, it is believed that the word comes from the Old English word "sterling," referring to the star on those coins.

As time marched on, the word became associated with silver of a quality equal to the standard English penny. To get down to the nitty-gritty, the word refers to alloys of 925 parts pure silver to 75 parts copper.

Today, of course, "sterling" has little to do with a coinage that seems to consist of one part silver to about a trillion parts ground-up beer cans and washing machine parts.

Q *My kid asked this the other day, and I'm stumped. Maybe Uncle Sol can help me out. Why do we call certain roads "highways"? Why isn't there a "lowway"?*

A Sol has often heard it said that the Pennsylvania Turnpike—once called the Ho Chi Minh Trail because of all the craters—could be renamed a "lowway." But that's another issue.

In reality, the "high" in highway has nothing to do with elevation. Instead, it refers to the fact that the first roads so named were primary roads, as opposed to little cow paths and rural lanes. According to the folks who put together the *Oxford English Dictionary,* the true opposite of "highway" is "byway," which refers to secluded, private, or unfrequented roads.

Q *Sol, every schoolchild knows that "Mr." is an abbreviation for "mister." But the dictionary doesn't have a word "missus." I'm confused.*

A You've hit on one of the great cover-ups of the English language. In polite company, "Mrs." is no longer an abbreviation, unless you're into regional abominations like the "missus" you mention.

The reason, of course, is that Mrs. is really short for "mistress," which is what married ladies used to be called before the term acquired a more off-color meaning. Nowadays, very few matrons of Sol's acquaintance would be happy to use the "Mrs." label under such circumstances.

All of this, of course, is another argument in favor of the generic "Ms."

Q *I've been thinking about lame ducks lately. What do politicians have to do with water fowl?*

A Nothing, except for their IQs. Ooops ... that just slipped out.

Originally, the term "lame duck" applied to businessmen who went belly-up, another graphic bit of terminology. The idea is that lame duck financiers, like their animal-kingdom counterparts, could only waddle out of the mess they had created. And not just waddle; they waddled with a limp.

As a political term, lame duck has a long and honorable history; it appears in a political context as early as 1840 referring to political leaders in the waning moments of their power.

Q *Recently, our synagogue had a white elephant sale, and I got to wondering: why do they call it a "white elephant"?*

A It all has to do with the fact that the stuff your temple is selling is stuff nobody with any sense wants anyway. It goes back to a Siamese legend that the king would give white elephants—sacred animals in this particular culture—to his enemies among the nobility.

Since these beasts were sacred, the unfortunate recipient would have to maintain the beast in the style to which it was accustomed. As a result, he would probably go broke caring for the animal.

So "white elephant" became synonymous with a gift that you were probably better off not getting. From there it was just a hop, skip, and a jump to identifying this allusion with charitable second-hand sales, where a good percentage of buyers soon rue their purchases.

Q *I've been to Jerusalem, but I didn't see any Jerusalem artichokes there. In fact, I didn't see any artichokes there. What gives?*

A Actually, there are two points to remember about Jerusalem artichokes. The first is that they don't come from Jerusalem, or anywhere close; the plants, known to people

who care about such things as *Helianthus tuberosus* of the Compositae family, are really indigenous to North America.

So why the "Jerusalem" in their name, you ask?

Apparently it's just a corruption of *girasole,* the Italian word for sunflower—a plant family that claims the Jerusalem artichoke as one of its own. Technically, the rubbery vegetable isn't even a real artichoke.

<hr/>

Q *Here's a good one for you: the symbols we use for numbers—1, 2, and all those—are referred to as "Arabic" numerals. But you can't fool me; I've been to Israel, and Arabic looks like spaghetti tracks left on paper. What gives?*

A You're nobody's fool, just a little confused; Arabs use regular numbers, just like plain old Americans. The fact that they're called "Arabic" is due to one of those curious whims of history.

In fact, Arabic numerals were derived from a number of sources, including Arabian and Hindu. They were introduced into Europe sometime in the tenth century, which is a good thing; prior to that, Europeans made due with awkward Roman numerals. Just try figuring the federal deficit in Roman numerals and see how far you get.

On second thought, maybe that's the way the government accountants keep their books. Let's see, now, CCXXXVVIII plus . . .

<hr/>

Q *This may sound trivial to you, but it's important to settle an argument: where does the word "nerd" come from? Is it Yiddish?*

A Why is it people assume that Yiddish is exclusively a language of humorous putdowns? Do you really think the *shtetl* was populated exclusively by wisecracking shmendricks and shnooks?

But nerd? The word is about as Yiddish as moo goo gai pan. According to the *American Heritage Dictionary,* the term derives from "nut," with an intermediate stop at "nurd," and if you believe that wholeheartedly, Sol would like to sell you a book describing how *you*, too, can buy a $50,000 luxury car confiscated from a drug dealer for only $1.59.

Sol's guess is that "nerd" is one of those terms that achieved popularity because it sounds exactly like what it describes. It's physically impossible to say it without sneering. Roll it around on your tongue a bit, and you can't help but picture some guy with bottle-bottom glasses, hunched up in front of a computer screen. You can't help but picture Sol, but that's another story.

Q *Sol, I was watching a baseball game the other day, and I got to wondering: why do we call left-handed pitchers "southpaws"? My own left hand faces a variety of positions, depending on which way I stand.*

A *Very* good, bubbe. Tomorrow we'll start work on tying your shoes.

The answer to your query is relatively straightforward. In most older baseball parks, the playing field is oriented so that the batter faces east—an effort to keep the poor buggers from staring into the late afternoon sun as they try to hit the silly little ball.

Most pitchers with any sense stand facing the batters, which puts their left hand vaguely in a southerly direction. Hence the term "southpaw," in case anybody other than you is interested.

Q *What is the origin of the word "yarmulke"? I asked my rabbi, and he was stumped.*

A Your rabbi was stumped for a very good reason; unfortunately, the guy who came up with the term "yarmulke" neglected to protect his trademark or write his memoirs, and thus failed to win a place of honor in the great trivia books of the world.

Over the years, various theories have attributed the root word to the Russians, the Turks, or the Germans. Other theorists have suggested that the word derives from the Hebrew—*yere malakhim*, which translates roughly to "feared kings." How this could have turned into "yarmulke," Sol cannot fathom.

Leo Rosten, the chief guru of Yiddish devotees the world over, traces it back to a Tartar word for "skullcap," which at least describes what it is. Others suggest the word came from the Latin word *almmucia*, a kind of Christian clerical head gear.

Of course, you could stay out of trouble and just use the Hebrew word *kippah*, and thus sound like something more than just a periodic bar mitzvah guest.

Q *Is Israel in the Near East or the Middle East? If it's either one, then where the heck is the other? And where is the*

East, for heaven's sake? And east of what? Do the Chinese or Japanese consider Israel to be in the West?

A My, we are busy little thinkers, aren't we? Next time you get the intellectual itch, lie down until it passes.

Let's start with the obvious; "Middle East" and other such constructions are relative terms that depend on who's doing the talking, and where they're talking from. After all, a plain old American could say with a degree of accuracy that Israel is in the West—the very *far* west. What goes around comes around, as some real shmendrick once said.

So such terms are a matter of convention, and these conventions change with changing perspectives.

In the days of the British Empire, for example, the Brits talked about just about anything east of the Mediterranean as "the East." When they wanted to get specific, they tended to refer to places like Palestine and the Arab countries as the "Near East," a term that still enjoys some popularity in our country, especially among the diplomatic set.

With the ascension of the United States in world affairs, the American term "Middle East" came into popular usage—so much so that now "Middle East" is the standard for the world. It's even used in Israel, the Arab countries, and China, which just shows how confused the Chinese really are, since Israel is to the west of the Mysterious Orient.

※

Q *Why do we call big shots "big wigs"? For that matter, why do we call them "big shots"?*

A When you talk about "big wigs," you're inadvertently referring to the practice in England, France, and other European locales of men wearing fancy wigs, which became stylish after Louis XIV lost his hair and began to wear a rug befitting his position—sort of like Dolly Parton with a liberal coating of white powder.

Other members of Louie's court decided it would be prudent to imitate the Big Enchilada, or the Big Croissant, as the case may be, and did so—with the more important functionaries wearing the biggest wigs, and so on.

And somehow, this quaint bit of folklore endured to the present time, when a guy in a cascading white wig would probably qualify for a rubber room, or a few guest shots on David Letterman.

"Big shot"? It comes from the world of gambling, and referred to high rollers at the craps table.

***

Q *Dear Sol: I always wondered why Jews call smoked salmon "lox," while the rest of the world calls it "smoked salmon."*

A Here we are, our species threatened with nuclear war and environmental catastrophe, and you're quibbling about why we call lox *lox*? Sheesh.

Basically, the Yiddish word "lox" derives from the German word for salmon, *der Seelachs*.

In the Christmas markets that dot Germany every December, some of the most popular stalls sell *Seelachs* sandwiches— bagels and lox, without the bagel and cream cheese. The lox is packed in a crusty roll stuffed with sliced onions.

In Norway, smoked salmon is called *lax*. Obviously, these guys were looking over each other's shoulders when they were inventing their languages.

Sol, like so many other Jews from the baby-boom years, used to puff up with pride as he watched America's space launches. There it was, for the whole world to see: America's space program was being fueled by a *Jewish food*. It said so right on the sides of those great rockets: "LOX in." Sol went into a tailspin when he learned that LOX was NASA-ese for liquid oxygen.

***

Q *Why do lawyers use "esquire" after their names? Is it because they think they're big shots?*

A Anecdotal evidence suggests that little boys, at some point in their lives, enjoy signing notes and letters with the word "esquire" after their names—a little prepubescent ego boost. If one were to be unkind to this most maligned of professions, one could argue that lawyers are simply people who have not quite outgrown this affectation.

In fact, the word derives from the Old French, meaning "shield bearer." In all its uses, it implies the concept of being a gentleman, an outmoded idea in this era of equal-opportunity rudeness. In the United States, the word has pretty much become the exclusive property of some lawyers, who apparently need the lift of a fancy ending to their names.

※

Q *Sol: Do you know bubkes? Just thought I'd ask.*

A If your question was meant to be insulting, think again; Answer Men have hides of steel. If you were asking if Sol knows Manny Bubkes, who used to sell aluminum siding in Teaneck, the answer is no.

Yiddish is an earthy language, and the Yiddish phrases that have made it into common American usage tend to be the earthiest of all.

The context in which "bubkes" is used usually makes its meaning crystal clear: "My parents went to Miami and didn't bring me bubkes." "You don't know bubkes about writing a funny newspaper column."

The word apparently stems from a Russian word for beans. In its original Yiddish usage, "bubkes" referred to goat feces—an unpleasant allusion, if one far from the experience of most American Jews.

Fortunately, Yiddish words sound so great—the insults, especially, hit with almost an audible *splat,* even when nobody knows exactly what they mean—that the connection to the literal meaning is usually lost in the mists of history.

Curiously, American teenagers are fond of a construction similar to the one you are asking about—except with the Anglo-Saxon expletive at the end, instead of bubkes. Get Sol's drift?

🌟

Q *Sol, I'm very confused. A while back, I was reading an old book, and it mentioned "marshmallows" as if they were derived from plants. Tell me, Sol, are marshmallows a kind of vegetable? My children will be delighted, and eagerly await your reply.*

A Sure, marshmallows are vegetables, and matzah balls grow on teeny shrubs found only in the backyards of certified grandmothers.

Do you seriously think that anything a four-year-old will eat without all kinds of *tsimmes* could possibly be good for the human body?

Originally, the term "marshmallow" referred to a plant known to more scholarly types as *Althaea officinalis,* a pink-flowered perennial herb which was once used to make a sweet, frothy confection and a medicinal tea that was supposed to cure hay fever.

But this is the twentieth century; anything nature does, we can do better with sugar, gelatin, and chemicals. The marsh-

mallows that drive your kids to a sugared-up frenzy have all the nutrition of cotton candy, and not a trace of *Althaea officinalis.*

✻

Q *Where does the word "okay" come from? What's the proper way to write it?*

A As far as Sol is concerned, "okay" is the most overused word in the English language, a fact that any parent of a teenager will understand. Sol prefers the more refined language of an earlier era, when "oh wow" filled gaps in conversation with taste and distinction.

But on to your question: "okay" owes its origin to that eminently forgettable president of the United States, Martin Van Buren, who served from 1837 to 1841. Van Buren was affectionately known to his admirers as "Old Kinderhook," after Kinderhook, New York, his home town.

Get it? OK? Politicians were really into descriptive titles in the old days, like "The Old Rail Splitter," and "Old Hickory." Somewhere along the merry jaunt of history, this custom was dropped; you'd never catch anyone calling George Bush "Old Kennebunkport," or Ron Reagan "The Old Snoozer."

But anyway, Van Buren's supporters came to abbreviate his nickname to "OK," and did things like chant these magic letters and wave "OK" placards to show their approval. Somehow, word of this triumph of human creativity spread and—*voilà*—"okay" became an almost universal term of approval.

The best way to write "okay" is to find some other word. In formal written communication, its use marks you as a college student—or worse.

✻

Q *Sol, I hesitate to ask this for fear of sounding ignorant. Most people use "bar mitzvah" as a verb, as in, "he's being* bar mitzvahed." *But in invitations and in my temple bulletin,*

people say things like, "so and so is becoming a bar mitzvah."
Why is this? Is it sheer pretentiousness?

A It's less pretentiousness than the plain fact that the editors of your temple bulletin are resisting the popular tendency to mangle the language. Ask any yuppie, a group who earnestly believe that their fancy college educations gave them license to mutilate the language with words like "impacting." Sol's team of semantic samurais groan in unison.

The same transformation has taken place for "bar mitzvah." What the words mean is "son of the commandment." It doesn't make any sense to say, "Little Schlomo is going to be sonned of the commandment."

Get the picture? If you want to be semantically correct, you should notify the world that little Schlomo is "becoming a bar mitzvah," as your synagogue does.

Of course, common semantic mistakes often catch on with the hoi polloi, and before the linguistic purists know it, these ungainly constructions become acceptable parts of the language. But Judaism, anchored as it is to ancient texts and to thousands of years' worth of tradition, seems more resistant to this mutation process.

⁂

Q *What, exactly, is a "crackpot"? I don't mean in the figurative sense, I mean literally. What is one's "pot," and how can it be "cracked"? Are right-wing crackpots any dumber than left-wing crackpots?*

A The origins of the term "crackpot" are a little unclear. In archaic usage, "pot" sometimes referred to the head, and "cracked" was, and is, a slang term for crazy. The two were natural partners, like lox and cream cheese.

In answer to your final query, Sol has always observed that right-wingers generally have pots every bit as cracked as their left-wing counterparts. The right-wingers are generally better dressed; left-wing crackpots appear to be more common in the Jewish tradition.

Let's call it a draw and forget the whole thing.

Q *I was re-reading an Isaac Bashevis Singer story, and I kept coming across the term "positivism." What does it mean, and is it anything like est?*

A No, bubbe, it's not like one of those self-help regimens that charge a lot for a weekend and won't let you go to the bathroom. This is philosophy we're talking about, the beef jerky of academic disciplines; you can chew on the stuff for a lifetime, and still not have the foggiest idea what it's made of.

Positivism, the system of philosophy devised by Auguste Comte back in the 1800s, says that the goal of knowledge is not to explain—but just to describe things that are observable and feelable.

Big deal, right? But that's the kind of stuff philosophers get paid for. And a few generations ago, many of our forebears in Eastern Europe expressed their intellectual estrangement from Judaism by embracing such ideas.

Positivists rejected the possibility of knowing the beginning and the end of anything, which, naturally, led to an uncomfortable relationship between positivists and religious leaders, whose daily grind is heavily into beginnings and endings.

Positivism enjoyed its heyday back in the golden age of scientific discovery, when people thought science would redeem mankind. Now, of course, we're more inclined to suspect science of inventing new diseases and wrecking the ozone layer. Positivism was particularly popular among Eastern European Jewish intellectuals in the last half of the nineteenth century.

Logical positivism is—Sol is simplifying here—pretty much the same thing, but with a lot of numbers.

Q *Sol, settle an argument for me. My wife says the twentieth century started on January 1, 1901. That's silly, I said it started on January 1, 1900. Who's right? A week's worth of dirty dishes is riding on your answer.*

A Get out your plastic gloves, friend: you blew it. The twentieth century technically began the first day of 1901; the year 1900 belonged to the nineteenth century. And the twenty-first, Sol is happy to report, will begin on the same date in 2001. In case you're interested, the current century, when it's all wrapped up, will have consisted of 36,525 days, 5,218 weeks, 25 leap years, and a partridge in a pear tree.

Jewish time, of course, figures things differently, but with the same degree of confusion. How else to explain the fact that Rosh Hashanah, the Jewish New Year, takes place in the seventh month of the religious or festival cycle?

Speaking of the upcoming Turn of the Century, Sol has been thinking lately about the implications of the dawn of the twenty-first century. Will businesses have to change their names? Will 20th Century-Fox have to move up a century, and spend billions of dollars changing their logos? Stay tuned.

Q *Where does the term "anti-Semitism" come from, and why doesn't it apply to other "Semites," like Arabs?*

A You're sharp as the proverbial tack; too bad you can't harness that intellectual dynamo you have there.

The term "anti-Semitism" was coined in 1879 by a German Jew hater, Wilhelm Marr. Marr was referring to the waves of anti-Jewish sentiment then sweeping across Europe, which he apparently supported.

As you point out, the Semitic people are commonly assumed to include the whole range of people living in the area of southwestern Asia, including Arabs and Jews. Actually, the designation technically deals with peoples that speak the Semitic family of languages—including Hebrew, Arabic, and a slew of now-forgotten ancient tongues.

But the term "anti-Semitism" applies strictly to bias against Jews, thanks to Herr Marr—and thanks to legions of Jew haters whose activities made it necessary for the world to coin a special word just for their brand of bigotry.

Q *Why do they call New York "Gotham"?*

A Sol has an answer for you, but if you're a devoted New Yorker, you're not going to like it.

"Gotham" was a term originally applied to a parish of Nottingham, England. The folks there were alleged to be a little on the stupid side, resulting in this sarcastic literary reference: the "wise men of Gotham."

Since that time, the idea has taken on a more generic meaning; it has come to refer to any place thought of as a "paradise for fools." Many cultures have enjoyed castigating some of their fellow citizens in this image.

New York became the American Gotham early in the nineteenth century, when Washington Irving stuck the name on the Big Apple. It is not exactly a flattering allusion.

And finally, the idea of an American Gotham was rejuvenated with the popularity of Batman, first as a comic book character, later as a television series and a big-budget movie. Batman's Gotham City was clearly a city of fools—and it bore a striking similarity to New York.

Holidays—Jewish and Otherwise

Q *I know Thanksgiving is not a Jewish holiday. But is it okay for Jews to celebrate it? I'm too old to give up turkey and stuffing.*

A Look, bubbe, Sol is no rabbi; for your personal spiritual counseling, Sol suggests you contact him/her at your earliest convenience. Sol doesn't do weddings, either, except as a guest and first in line at the food table.

But perhaps some light can be shed on Thanksgiving. Its origins are Christian, and over the years Christian trappings have clung to the day—along with football, Maalox, and giant Mickey Mouse balloons.

But Thanksgiving was also influenced by Jewish history. The classic American Holiday derives from the Pilgrims, who did more than just wear funny hats; they came to these shores after fleeing religious persecution. Records show that these immigrants felt a certain kinship with the Jews of the Bible, who fled slavery in Egypt.

Officially, Thanksgiving became a major American holiday in 1863, when President Lincoln designated the last Thursday in November for the annual Turkey Day rite.

Judaism, of course, has its own day of thanks for the bounty of the harvest—Sukkot, called in the Bible the "harvest festival." Small world, isn't it?

In case you're not fully aware of it, the "harvest" includes things like grains, fruits, and vegetables—not Doritos and Hostess Ho Hos. Just thought you'd like to know.

Q *It's almost Pesach, and I had a terrible thought: the canned dog food that my Toodles likes so much contains corn meal and wheat by-products. Does this mean it's* chametz, *and that I have to let the poor pooch starve?*

A Sol has never cared for dogs, so he's striving mightily to find a particle of sympathy for your Toodles. Because the fact is, *chametz* is *chametz,* and if it's in your house during Passover, it's bad news for that beast of yours.

In case you come from some other planet and are unaware of the rituals of Passover, *chametz* refers to any leavened product, or any product made with wheat, rye, oats, or barley—except for matzah, the unleavened bread specified in the Bible. During Passover, Jews are supposed to rid their homes of every scrap of *chametz,* or at least technically relinquish ownership of the stuff.

As for your dog food, your only option, according to Sol's vast team of rabbinic advisers, is to sell the *chametz* to a non-Jew, along with all the other *chametz* in your house. During Pesach you'll have to keep the pooch food locked up and feed your canine companion something else.

If you have questions about your pet's health, look for an observant Jewish veterinarian—admittedly, not the easiest thing to find. Sol has heard of one religious veterinarian who dispenses advice about what to feed all kinds of animals during Pesach, from mutts like Toodles to pet eels.

Personally, Sol doesn't see anything wrong with feeding the creature a steady diet of Valium, but that's another story.

Q *I don't suppose there's much hope, but can you think of any Jewish slant on Valentine's Day? My kids really like those cute little cards.*

A You know that old saying about a "snowball's chance in heck," as we say in the family magazine business?

St. Valentine's day has a checkered history, not a lick of it Jewish.

The holiday began as a Roman fertility rite. In a tradition your kids would recognize, the names of the young girls of Rome were put into a box and drawn by the boys—who probably fudged it, the way kids do today. Being a fertility rite, the process involved a few things a little less innocent than pretty hearts glued onto doilies.

When the Christians came along, they tried to stamp out the erotic content of the "day for lovers" by assigning it to a saint, taking out the fertility rituals, and re-defining it as a day celebrating innocent romantic love. St. Valentine was a Roman priest in the third century who was best known for converting pagans to Christianity. For his trouble, he got himself condemned, executed, and sainted, the religious equivalent of the hat trick in hockey. So the date of his execution—February 14—was assigned as his in perpetuity.

The amorous character of St. Valentine's Day in our era has nothing to do with Valentine, who was, after all, a saint, not a lover. Nor was he known as a profligate giver of Whitman's Samplers. But Church leaders had given up trying to suppress the pagan holidays; instead, they just gave the old fetes new meanings. So the old fertility feast and St. Valentine's Day were melded, and the rest is history.

Should Jewish kids participate in St. Valentine's Day?

Sol suggests you consult your local rabbi. Most Reform rabbis don't make a big deal about it; many in the Orthodox community shun Valentine's Day as an alien religious holiday.

Q *What is a hobgoblin? Where did the word originate? What is the Orthodox view of Halloween?*

A Halloween is a big headache for just about every major religion, unless you consider paganism a major religion.

To take your questions in order, a casual exploration of the ever-helpful *Oxford Universal Dictionary* reveals that "hobgoblin" is just another name for "Robin Goodfellow," a particularly nasty sprite.

Halloween, the reason we know about goblins, is a contraction of "All Hallows' Eve, or "All Saints' Eve—a bad sign, as far as Jewishness goes. In pagan tradition, this falls on the last day of October, a day when the witches and imps

cavort. In those days, the event had a slightly more sinister meaning than a bunch of little Cinderellas and Supermen gorging themselves on chocolate and lollypops.

The whole shmeer was incorporated into Christianity in the ninth century, another example of early Christianity's impressive "If you can't lick 'em, join 'em" philosophy.

Interestingly, the pumpkin, that universal symbol of the day, isn't so universal after all; until Halloween was brought to America, the vegetable symbol of Halloween was a carved turnip. Just try hacking a grinning face on one of *those*.

As for the Jewish angle on Halloween, many Orthodox people today refuse to allow their children to participate in the festivities, because of its connections to alien religions. Reform leaders make a big deal about Purim costumes—but in the end, many concede that the allure of Halloween is too strong to resist, especially for candy-crazed 10-year-olds.

Q *Sol, can you give me the scoop on a rumor I've heard for years? It goes like this: Coca-Cola connoisseurs always load up on the product during Passover—because they say it tastes like Coke used to taste. What gives?*

A Sol is continually amazed by the number of people who talk about Coca-Cola in terms of vintages. For this strange breed, they stopped making "real" Coke about the time tailfins disappeared from cars.

In fact, for a number of years now, Coke has used corn syrup, a sweetener that purists contend does not have the smooth taste, not to mention the fine bouquet, of true cane or beet sugar.

But during Pesach, many Jews refrain from eating corn, as well as your basic bread and stuff. This poses a major headache for food manufacturers; to certify their products for Passover use, they must remove a whole list of ingredients derived from corn—including stabilizers, corn oil, and the ubiquitous and inexpensive corn syrup.

In Coke and Pepsi, the corn syrup is replaced for a short time by cane and beet sugar, which means the stuff tastes more like it did when you were a kid. The changeover costs both companies several hundred thousand dollars every year.

Of course, for those of us with less refined palates, new Coke, old Coke, Passover Coke, it's all the same.

☀

Q *Sol, if laws are laws and* Halachah *is* Halachah, *then why can Sephardim eat some things at Passover and Ashkenazim can not? And vice versa, of course. And more importantly, who's right? Of course the Ashkenazim think they are, but who truly is the arbiter of taste, so to speak?*

A Okay, let's sort out this tangle without stepping on religious sensibilities. To begin with, while there may be disagreement about some of the finer points of the dietary laws, there is no such agreement about the basics. You won't find any Orthodox groups chowing down at, say, Porky's Original Southern Barbecue stand because of some idiosyncratic rabbinic ruling, or slugging down oysters at a neighborhood raw bar.

But the interpretation of the law—secular and religious—is not entirely clear on every last point, which is why we have lawyers and rabbis. Look at the bright side: rabbis deal with a vastly more complex code of law, and they don't even make you ransom your first-born child, the way lawyers do.

So, for instance, Ashkenazic Jews do not eat legumes (or corn products, to some, a legume) during Passover because of the possibility that things like corn flour might accidentally be used in the making of Passover matzah; only five grains can be used in the baking of Passover matzah, and flour made from things like corn and rice isn't among them.

But Sephardic rabbis have ruled that nothing in Jewish law actually prohibits the consumption of legumes during Passover. These sages of old apparently were not so concerned about confusion in the kitchen.

Who's right? Look, bubbe, Sol may sound a little meshuga at times, but he's not that meshuga.

Q *How do you observe Passover if you're in a country that doesn't allow the importation or use of wine, and you don't want to risk smuggling any in? Please, nothing so simple as, "Just leave the country."*

A From time immemorial, Jews have been masters of "make do," an adaptability that goes hand in glove with living in the midst of hostile societies.

So what do you do if you're in a place where Mogen David Extra-Sweet has yet to make an appearance, and the local *federales* forbid wine? No sweat: no nation known to Sol outlaws grape juice, which will do just fine for ritual purposes.

Along these lines, the Lubavitch organization, which turns up in some pretty strange places, held a seder in Nepal a while back. Nepal, a largely Hindu country, does not allow the importation of wine; the Chabad people, undaunted as usual, merely flew in enough grape juice to take care of the seder.

Q *Sol, why aren't there any Jewish holidays in the summer? Was it that in the old days, the rabbis were all off basking on the beaches?*

A Rabbis? Basking? You must be kidding. And, to be honest, your question indicates a somewhat limited knowledge of the Jewish calendar; in fact, there are several important dates in the summer, besides your annual Ocean City debauch.

Shavuot comes seven weeks from the second day of Passover, which turns out to be just around Memorial Day—pretty near summer vacation, the way most people look at things. Tisha B'Av comes at the end of July, the ninth of Av, a definite inconvenience for beach-going rabbis. The end of summer coincides with the important time of preparation for the High Holy Days.

It should also be pointed out that many major Jewish holidays coincide with the planting and harvest cycles, activities that are at a minimum in the middle of summer. But the bottom line, at least for observant Jews, is that the holidays are distributed through the calendar according to God's plan, not rabbis' vacation plans.

Q *Sol: Every year around Passover, I hear this debate over whether store-bought matzah is good enough. What's your opinion?*

A If it's a religious ruling you're looking for, you're barking up the wrong tree, bubbe. In centuries to come, it is highly unlikely that commentators on Jewish affairs will say things like, "According to Reb Sol . . ."

Your query brings up a matter of opinion—quite heated opinion, in some cases.

The biggest complaint among some Orthodox Jews is that matzah-making machinery, being mere machinery, could result in dough lingering unbaked somewhere en route to the ovens. The delay could cause a smidgen of fermentation, something forbidden on Passover.

So some Orthodox people reject matzah made in big factories in faraway places, which are harder to supervise and where the matzah cannot be watched at every stage in the process. Groups like the Lubavitchers prefer baking their own, rushing the matzah into the ovens, and washing cooking implements frequently to avoid fermentation.

In the eyes of many Orthodox, their own old-fashioned efforts are less likely to result in even a minor violation of the Pesach regulations. You can't be too careful, they argue.

Most Reform and Conservative Jews take the position that machine-made matzah certified kosher for Passover is perfectly acceptable; any minute traces of fermentation, they argue, would hardly violate the spirit of Passover.

Q *Can a Jew work as a department store Santa Claus?*

A What's wrong, you couldn't get a job selling ties or something?

The whole issue of Christmas is a tough one for many Jews. In this country, the holiday has sometimes taken on secular qualities that make it seem about as sacred as Groundhog Day.

But the holiday is a deeply religious one for many Christians. And, more specifically, the modern Santa Claus character was based on a saint, for crying out loud; if this isn't a Christian symbol, Sol doesn't know what is.

The modern Santa Claus is based on Saint Nicholas, who performed miracles and became the patron saint of sailors back in the fourth century. Reportedly, old St. Nick was a generous soul, particularly to children—the apparent origin of today's Santa Claus legend.

To the Orthodox among us, this is a serious matter; even loose associations with the religious symbols of another religion are taboo. A while back, more Reform-minded leaders tended to look the other way when it came to the secularized symbols of Christmas; lately, the pendulum seems to be swinging back the other way.

Q *Okay, see if you can follow this, Sol. New Year's Eve is a big deal in New York, with that garish globe coming down at the stroke of midnight. And New York is a heavily Jewish city. So why don't they perform a similar ritual for the Jewish New Year? Seems to me that it would be a politically expedient thing to do.*

A Sol can see it all now: Times Square at 11:59 on a warm September night, crowds of people in *kippahs*, a big illuminated bagel slowly descending to the street . . .

Sorry to dash your dreams, but such a scene would be a little inappropriate. New Year's Eve in the secular world has become a symbol of uninhibited celebration, if not debauchery; in fact, the tradition, which has its origins in ancient times, is essentially a pagan one.

Later, Christian society attempted to co-opt the holiday by portraying it as the day of Jesus' circumcision.

But in the Jewish calendar, Rosh Hashanah is a sober, thoughtful occasion—the beginning of the Ten Days of Penitence ending with Yom Kippur.

The emphasis is on introspection and repentance, not on champagne and idiotic noisemakers.

Remember: the High Holidays are known as the Days of Awe. It's hard to imagine giving a name like that to an event that involved listening to Dick Clark count backwards to midnight.

꙳

Q *Sol, if we celebrate Chanukah because one night's supply of oil burned for eight days, shouldn't Chanukah really be a seven-night celebration? After all, there was enough oil for one night, so that's not a miracle. The miracle would be the other seven days. What say the grand poobahs of* Halachah *and holidays?*

A Sol ran this one by a rabbi, who groaned at the prospect of answering it one more time; you're not cutting any new trails here, bubbe.

Still, your question is not an uninteresting one, especially since the eight nights of Chanukah represent about the longest stretch of sustained interest in religion that many American Jews can manage. On the other hand, maybe it's just the presents.

There are actually a number of different explanations for the fact that we celebrate all eight nights.

Sol presumes that he need not remind you that Chanukah commemorates the victory of the Maccabees over the forces of Antiochus Epiphanes, and the miracle that took place in the rebuilt Temple, where a small amount of oil burned for eight days.

According to one interpretation, the first night of the holiday celebrates the fact that the Maccabees found a cruse of consecrated oil in the first place; the other nights celebrate the miraculous fact that the oil lasted.

Another explanation suggests that the Maccabees set an eight-day celebration because Solomon had done the same in the First Temple. Still another has the first day serving as a celebration for the victory over the Greeks and their Syrian henchmen, the other days for the miracle of the oil.

Still another explanation suggests that the Maccabees found eight spears inside the Temple when they booted the Syrian-Greek forces out—which they planted in the ground and used as a kind of giant menorah.

There are more theories, but you get the idea.

Strange Science and Technology

Questions Too Hot for Mr. Wizard

Q *Sol, why is it that the flu seems to originate in the Far East? I mean there's the Hong Kong and the Asian and the Singapore flus. Does any flu come from, say, Israel? Or Kalamazoo—you know, the "Kalamazoo Flu"?*

A *You* wanna write this column? Sol doesn't like people hogging the best lines, if you'll forgive the unkosher allusion.

But on to your question. Many flu strains originate in the Far East for a very good reason. Unfortunately, scientists haven't figured out what it is yet. Several epidemiologists consulted by this Answer Man responded with the scientists' equivalent of "huh?"

But it is known that many strains of this unpleasant class of diseases originate in China. That isn't to say that the Chinese have a monopoly on these nasty things; Sol's favorite is the Ann Arbor strain, the symptoms of which include headache, fever, and an irresistible tendency to go on panty raids.

Another bit of absolutely useless information: in the Southern Hemisphere, flu strikes in July and August—winter in those climates. Obviously, there's a connection between flu epidemics and cold weather. So when your mom *hoks* you about wearing a warm sweater and your mittens, believe her.

Sol invites his loyal readers to contribute any halfway-plausible explanations for the medical version of the China Syndrome. The most ridiculous contributions will be promptly forwarded to the Centers for Disease Control, where they should fit in just fine. Please, no conspiracy theories about Red Chinese germ warfare labs or anything like that.

Q *Sol, what happens to all the wax after Chanukah candles are burned? There's nothing left. That doesn't happen to my romantic dining room candles, which drip in pretty artistic patterns.*

A Sol can just picture your dining room: dusty old wine jugs with candles stuck in the top, maybe a blinking neon sign and

a Lava Lamp, a place with all the class of Wendy's at high noon.

It is baffling to Sol, whose interest in science is limitless, that even Jews, to whom candles are an important part of ritual life, have a fundamental misunderstanding of the physics of these clever inventions.

Answer honestly: do you have the faintest idea of what function wax serves, besides just getting your tablecloth all glopped up?

The plain facts are these. When you light the wick of a candle—a Shabbat candle, a Chanukah candle, or a candle stuck in any empty Perrier bottle—you cause the wax at the top of the candle to melt. The molten wax, in turn, is drawn up, wicked up, if you will, through capillary action in the fibers of the wick.

It's the combustion of the evaporated wax vapor that produces the steady, intense flame.

Candle wax is, in fact, a blend of a variety of ingredients, including paraffin wax and stearic acid. Varying those ingredients can produce candles that vaporize and burn with almost no residue—or candles that leave wax drippings that some people find artistic.

Which, as any Jewish homemaker can tell you, is the last thing you want all over your menorah.

Also, the waxless candle more accurately mimics the oil lamps, which some very Orthodox Jews still insist is the only appropriate light for the Festival of Lights.

🕎

Q *When I see a full moon, does the rest of the world see it?*
A One of the instructive aspects of being an Answer Man is the opportunity to become familiar with the depths of human ignorance. Your question is a shining example.

Let's take this real slow. When you are gazing at the full moon, do you know what folks in, say, China, see? The sun, bubbe. The moon is not visible to all parts of the earth at the same time, for the same reason that you don't see stuff very well behind your own head, unless you're a schoolteacher.

Are you following? Now perhaps what you are asking is whether folks in Baltimore see a full moon, while people in, say, San Francisco see only a crescent on the same night. Wrong again; the phases of the moon have nothing to do with where on earth you are when you happen to see them.

The phases of the moon are caused by the relative position of the three bodies in question—the sun, the moon, and the earth. When the moon is directly between its two heavenly comrades, it is invisible, the phase called the "new moon." Put that idea in the hands of a Madison Avenue type, and you might end up with a "new and *improved* moon." It has a nice ring to it, *nu?*

Anyway, as the moon continues its orbit around the earth, only a sliver of the rocky chunk is illuminated, at least as far as viewers on earth are concerned. The full moon becomes visible when the moon is on the *other* side of the earth, relative to the sun. Got it?

The leisurely journey of earth's little buddy is nice for people who write doggerel verse, but it's also important to Jews. This cycle is the basis of the lunar calendar on which the Jewish calendar is based; without the phases of the moon, the rabbis of old would have had a heck of a time knowing when to celebrate what.

Q *Do cats get headaches?*

A At first, Sol misunderstood and assumed you were asking a question with an all-too-obvious answer—*are* cats headaches?

But on reflection, it's obvious you're referring to cats as sufferers of this affliction, not as causes. And in that regard, the answer is, alas, not a simple one.

On one hand, Sol's veterinary consultants insist that cats have all the physical concomitants of headaches, including the kinds of vascular contraction and expansion that cause migraines in humans, primarily parents of human teenagers.

Researchers in England studied cats who sleep on top of television sets, and are thereby affected by the radiations of the set, not to mention the commercials. The researchers concluded that brain-wave patterns in these beasts show changes in electrical activity suggestive of headaches. No doubt these headaches got worse during "Wheel of Fortune."

On the other hand, our feline friends are highly reticent about expressing their feelings on the headache issue; it's difficult to ascertain with any reliability that a cat's ill temper is the result of Excedrin Headache Number 3, or merely the result of the lousy disposition to which the species is subject.

So to answer your question, yes, cats probably do get headaches—but not as many as they cause.

Q *Sol, where do fruit flies come from? When I buy a banana, I don't see the critters. Do they come in from my screens, or is this some weird form of spontaneous generation?*

A You can take your imagination out of overdrive; in fact, the answer is much grosser than spontaneous generation.

The little critters come from eggs deposited in the fruit long

before it hits your grimy pantry. The fly larvae feed on the pulp of the fruit, or on yeasts that grow on the same stuff you will eventually cram into your mouth. If the fruit sits around long enough, the larvae turn into flies, and the result are those gnat-like things that always seem to be hovering about a millimeter in front of your eyeball.

Q *How much caffeine does it take to kill a person?*

A Long-term or short-term? Long-term, of course, the jury is still out on caffeine, although the substance, a natural component of coffee, tea, and chocolate, and added to a wide variety of foods and medicines, is clearly related to problems like hypertension.

Short-term, it takes a lot of caffeine to produce toxic effects. If you're planning on using caffeine to shuck this mortal coil, Sol suggests you re-think your plans; depending on a person's size and general physical condition, it would

take between 90 and 110 cups of coffee over a three-to four-hour period.

Thanks to coffee's diuretic qualities, after the first 10 cups or so you'd be too busy trotting off to the you-know-what to finish the job, not to mention the fact that you'd be shaking too much to get the cup to your trembling lips.

Q *With the leaves off the trees, I've noticed large, round clumps of leaves about 12 inches in diameter. Are these nests of some sort, and who lives in these abodes?*

A The nest you describe is the ornithological equivalent of an abandoned building, bubbe. According to the nature buffs at the Smithsonian Institution, it most likely once belonged to a family of orioles. But, sensible birds that they are, they split for warmer climes when the leaves started falling—leaving behind their characteristic leafy nests, which are stuck together with bits of string, hairs, and other urban detritus.

The secret Smithsonian informant also felt compelled to add that some species, most notably the cliff swallow, actually use spit as an adhesive to hold their nests together, which just goes to show that people aren't the only species with gross habits.

Q *Solly, why don't you find cockroaches in cars? Do they get motion sick or something?*

A Motion-sick cockroaches? There's such a thing as carrying this nature stuff too far.

Cockroaches have distinct preferences when it comes to environments and generally speaking, cars are not near the top of their list, even if yours looks like a mobile dump site.

Our hard-shelled friends generally like their living quarters warm, moist, and stable. With all those wonderful kitchens

around, why would they even think of nesting in your car, which is freezing in the winter, scorching in the summer, fairly dry, and probably fairly devoid of food sources?

Q *Why do slugs disintegrate when you sprinkle salt on them?*

A This is a favorite question for Answer Men, sort of the scientific equivalent of "What was Lucy and Ricky's address?"

But for those readers with an interest in this kind of dreck, the answer is as follows: this bizarre form of pest control works because these gross beasts don't have much in the way of skin to protect them from the dehydration that salt causes.

So—*poof*—they just sort of shrivel up and disintegrate when faced with a salvo from your saltshaker.

But this leads to another question: what does Jewish law, which has such an emphasis on the humane treatment of animals, say about nasty things like slugs and cockroaches?

In fact, Jewish law *does* allow the killing of vermin; the important distinction is between animals that disturb a person's functioning, and those that don't.

In other words, if you're grossed out by slugs to the point where you're getting a little crazy, a traditional Jewish view is that it's okay to do the salt trick. If they don't upset your functioning, you'd best let the buggers live.

Q *Is it true that horses never vomit, and that if they get a stomach illness you have to walk them for hours or they'll die? This has been bugging me. It's important, because if horses don't really give a "Technicolor yawn," we could create a new expression: it's enough to make a horse vomit.*

A A Technicolor yawn? You've grossed Sol to the max, bubbe. You must be a mother of small kids or something, and used to stomach-turning experiences.

But never let it be said that your neighborhood Answer Man ducks the tough ones. According to people far more authoritative than Sol, horses do indeed lack the musculature to vomit. A lot of people don't believe this, because when horses gag on their feed they cough a lot and have—in the unforgettable words of one equine expert—a "profuse foamy effusion." This might just fool the uninitiated into thinking it was the "Technicolor yawn" to which you so graphically alluded.

What veterinarians do with horses who get unpleasant things stuck in their throats is massage the esophagus, or use a syringe to force oil or water down the murky passageway to carry the material into the beast's stomach. Since horses can't vomit, their own futile efforts to dislodge foreign materials can rip up the lining of their throats and lead to serious infection.

Q *I heard this absolutely unbelievable rumor that the EPA was thinking about banning rice at weddings—the throwing of rice, not the eating. Is this another example of government interference run wild?*

A Don't panic; the EPA doesn't care if you litter the sidewalks with uncooked rice.

The question of lethal rice is not entirely clear. Some environmentalists believe that our feathered friends are quite grateful for the rice people throw at newlyweds—until the uncooked stuff absorbs water in their innards, swells, and . . . but you don't want to know the gory details.

But others, including that all-purpose authority Ann Landers, argue that uncooked rice is basically harmless.

Interestingly, the throwing of things at newlyweds to symbolize fertility is almost universal. In Jewish tradition, barley and wheat were the favored grains; ancient Oriental civilizations, naturally, preferred rice.

Q *Why do ostriches bury their heads in the sand? Is this a sign of their limited intelligence, or does it really work for them?*

A Do you believe everything you're told, bubbe? Did you hear that Sol won the Brooklyn Bridge in the lottery—and has a special offer, just for you?

The plain fact is, ostriches react to danger just like any other animal with a modicum of good sense: they run. Do you honestly think they'd have survived this long if their best response to danger was sticking their head in the ground? In fact, they can run like all get out, and when cornered, they can defend themselves pretty effectively with those strange-looking legs.

The literary allusion probably stems from the fact that their long necks and little heads suggest overwhelming stupidity. But as Charles Darwin taught, you don't need to be an Einstein to survive, just good instincts.

Q *Is it true that lightning never strikes in the same place twice?*

A This falls into the wishful thinking category—the idea if your house gets zapped once, it's immune from then on.

In fact, the probability of getting hit once, twice, or a

thousand times is directly related to your location. If you're in an apartment in Baltimore, the odds of even a single lightning strike are minuscule; if you live at the top of the Sears Tower in Chicago, the chances are pretty good.

Probability is very similar to religion in some respects; some of its teachings require a leap of faith in order to be grasped by ordinary folks.

So the probability theorists would tell us that the odds of lightning striking a second time are exactly the same as the probability of the first strike, a concept that almost nobody really believes.

Q *How come flies can walk on the ceiling?*

A This cosmic mystery has puzzled scientists and housewives for generations. In the old days, it was thought that the pesky critters had suction mechanisms in their feet; they clung to the ceiling because of miniature Hoovers, so to speak.

In fact, flies decorate your ceiling because you don't have screens on your windows, and, besides that, because they have fleshy glandular pads on their feet. These pads, or *pulvilus,* secrete sticky goop that lets them stick to your nice white ceilings. They also have claws, an adaptation that allows them to walk on stucco ceilings, too.

Q *Here's one that'll stump you, big shot. Why does water boil funny in a microwave oven?*

A By "boil funny," Sol takes it you are referring to the tendency of water heated in a microwave to erupt in a sudden *woosh.* You talk sort of funny, too, which may mean that your microwave is leaking right into the old noggin.

But you are correct about the difference between boiling water on a stove and zapping it.

On a stove, the water is heated from the bottom up—no great surprise. Heat is also conducted by the sides of the container. Since warmed water rises continuously, you get a constant flow of warmer water to the surface, where people with nothing better to do watch it.

In a microwave, everything from Lean Cuisine to your basic H_2O is heated from the middle. When you stop to consider it, this is a question of almost Talmudic complexity; how can something be heated from the inside out, without the *outside* getting hot while the stuff *doing* the heating is busy getting *inside*? It's no accident that "metaphysics" and "physics" are linguistic kissing cousins.

So: water heated from the inside rises, but the cooler water around it is busy sinking. So what you get is a big pocket of hotter water gradually working its way to the surface until—presto—the great hiccup that indicates that your water is hot enough to brew tea.

Q *How does the heat pump for my house work? The repairman says it extracts heat from the outside air when it's cold. This strikes me as silly, since if there was any heat outside on a cold day, I'd feel it. Is this just a trick?*

A Do you sense that people are plotting against you? Do you hear Z-106 over your tooth fillings?

The sensible answer to your question is that heat pumps, which allegedly provide high-efficiency heating and air con-

ditioning for many modern American homes, are like so many things in life: they can be understood only after a considerable leap of faith.

If there was no heat outside, you think it would only be 19 degrees or so? You bet your life it wouldn't; no heat at all implies something like absolute zero, which is colder even than Minneapolis.

So—believe Solly—there's heat, even if you feel like Nanook of the North. What your heat pump does is extract it, by working like a kind of refrigerator in reverse. In your basic fridge, you have coils on the bottom, which are warm and insulated by at least an inch of dust. You also have coils in the inside, which are cold, and a lot of Freon in the pumping system that connects the two.

Here's where it gets tricky. The Freon moves back and forth between a liquid and a gaseous state. Every time it performs this neat trick, it either releases heat or sucks it up. It makes this change with the aid of a compressor, a device with a life expectancy of approximately 16 hours.

The same process is at work in your heat pump. In the summer, the device pulls heat from your house and transfers it outside; in the winter, it finds those elusive degrees in the chilly outside air, and transforms them into heat to keep you nice and toasty.

Now if they could only apply the same principle to dust . . .

Q *Sol, if people are living longer, why is the onset of puberty occurring earlier and earlier? I mean, it's not like we have to have kids at 13 because life expectancy is 35. Shouldn't a worried mom be able to relax for an extra year or two?*

A A good point, buttercup. Nobody knows precisely why kids hit this hideous milestone at an ever-earlier age. A lot of it has to do with nutrition; the earlier onset of puberty appears to be a Western phenomenon, correlated to three squares a day supplemented by Big Macs and fries.

But there is also speculation that some of the problem, which transforms tranquil, sweet children into glandular monsters, may be related to the hormones in things like beef, which stimulate the pituitary glands to accelerate the awful process.

Incidentally, the average age for the onset of puberty is a matter of some dispute. Some of Sol's most trusted reference books put the figure at somewhere between 11 and 14 for girls, 12 and 16 for boys. But some doctors suggest that parents are in serious trouble even earlier—at 8 to 10 for girls, 9 to 14 for boys.

Q *Did Jews invent antacids? It would seem natural, since so many Jews seem to have ulcers.*

A Guess again, bubbe; you're off-target on both issues.

Statistically speaking, Jews don't get ulcers any more than any other group. And despite the widespread perception that ulcers are the exclusive preserve of white-collar toilers, the fact is that poverty is an even greater correlate of the dread digestive grunge. The only difference is that upper-class folks seem to take a perverse pride in their ulcers—as if Maalox was a badge of their hard working natures.

As for antacids, they were invented by the ancient Sumerians, who uncovered some of the secrets of baking soda long before Arm & Hammer. Sodium bicarbonate, they discovered early on, could offset the unsettling effects of too much grass and twigs in the diet. Nowadays, we use the same thing for too many potato chips and Twinkies.

Q *How did people ever figure out that microwaves could cook stuff? Was it all a dreadful accident?*

A It was lucky for Percy LeBaron Spencer that it wasn't more of an accident than it was. Spencer, an employee of the

Raytheon Company, was working with a magnetron tube, a key component of some radar systems that produces electromagnetic energy in the microwave range.

But at snack time, Spencer discovered that the chocolate bar in his pocket had melted. He assumed the obvious—that microwave radiation from his magnetron had somehow cooked the chocolate, without producing any noticeable heat.

Being the curious sort, Spencer did some further experimentation—with popcorn and eggs. And the rest, as they say, is history.

Q *What do they do with all the fat in milk when they make skim milk?*

A What's your problem? Has your delicate palate never encountered fine Velveeta cheese? Sheesh, don't you read labels on packages?

The fact is, there are about a billion things clever food manufacturers do with the fat skimmed from your basic high-fat milk, things that hide beneath generic-sounding names like "milk-fat solids." The aforementioned Velveeta, which Sol thinks has received a bad rap in recent years, is just one example.

Q *Why do seagulls hang around in parking lots? What do they think they are, teenagers?*

A Ha, another comedian. Seagulls generally prefer to hang around water. In the absence of water, however, they seek out other flat, open areas—which, in your average city, means a parking lot.

It's also true that seagulls, like teenagers, are notoriously un-fussy about what they eat. Urban parking lots, with their ever present fast-food detritus, are thus doubly attractive to the pesky birds.

Q *Can word processors write in Hebrew? It would be a great help in my Hebrew School work.*

A What's wrong, you think a machine that can play games like "Ninja Sadists from Pluto" can't handle a simple language like Hebrew?

A number of word processing packages can fly through Hebrew with blinding speed. Reading right to left is a serious headache for humans; for computers and the correct software, it's a byte out of a piece of cake.

Be forewarned, however, that you will need a graphics card in your computer and a dot matrix or laser printer. And, of course, a knowledge of Hebrew in your head; advanced technology has not yet conquered the problem of actually learning the language for us.

※

Q *Sol, how do those crazy pump toothpaste tubes work? I took one apart recently to see what makes it tick, and I'm darned if I can figure it out.*

A These toothpaste gizmos represent the pinnacle of American ingenuity; with an effort only slightly less massive than the Manhattan Project, scientists and engineers have finally solved one of the great problems of our age—the shnooks who squeeze regular toothpaste tubes from the middle, instead of the end.

These pump containers are constructed of several elements. The assembly at the top is a small pump, with a flapper valve. Directly beneath this valve, which is not unlike the flapper in your toilet, is the cylinder that holds your toothpaste. At the bottom of the cylinder is a little disk keeping the stuff from dripping out all over your counter.

When you push the button, it squeezes out everything in the top section—air and some toothpaste. When you release the button, the flapper valve opens and the vacuum draws more toothpaste into the pump assembly.

The really neat thing is the way the little disk on the bottom rises as the level of toothpaste diminishes. This is due primarily to atmospheric pressure, according to Sol's engineering advisers. And if you believe that, maybe Sol can interest you in his very own money-market fund.

Q *Sol, I have a physics question for you. When I put my husband's underwear in the washing machine right-side out, why do they come out of the washer inside out? This is causing double work for me and is quite frustrating. Are these laundry* dybbuks?

A You call questions about inside-out underwear *physics?* Next think you know, you'll be talking about ironing as philosophy.

To provide a halfway-plausible answer, Sol attempted to replicate your underwear results in his own washer, a state-of-the-art job with a wringer and everything. When that produced no inside-out skivvies, Sol proceeded to attempt the experiment again on a Westinghouse front loader.

Sure enough, out of 10 pairs of flimsies, 9 reversed themselves. Men's, women's, kids', it made no difference; obviously, the agitation and tumbling through the circular motion of the washer drum created forces that handily reversed the underwear.

But remember: underwear is particularly easy to turn inside out. The same cannot be said of, say, men's T-shirts—only a small proportion of which underwent this particular transformation. And long-sleeved shirts exhibited no such propensity, for obvious reasons.

The answer to your dilemma, buttercup, is obvious: turn the underwear inside out before you put it in the washer. Nine times out of ten, according to Sol's advanced scientific experimentation, they'll come out ready to wear.

Q *My dad takes nitroglycerin tablets for his heart. Do I need to be concerned about the possibility that he might explode?*

A No need to worry, there's no danger a good slap on the back will turn old Abba into a Fourth of July display.

Nitroglycerin, which was discovered in 1846 by an Italian scientist, is indeed one of the most explosive substances known to this explosive-happy species.

The nitroglycerin that comes in pharmacy vials is the same stuff, but it has been stabilized with all kinds of fillers, like lactose, so it can do its good job as a vasodilator—in English, something that opens up blood vessels plugged up from too many lunches at Hardees.

Although not explosive, nitroglycerin tablets are chemically unstable, and in time the nitro evaporates, leaving just the filler. So Sol's pharmaceutical advisers urge patients who use the stuff to have their prescriptions refilled at the recommended intervals.

❋

Q *Dear Sol: Why does your nose run when it's cold outside?*

A Are you really sure you want to get into this subject?

Your shnoz is lined with mucous glands, a fact that Sol is sure gives you great pleasure. These produce the stuff that makes your five-year-old a disgusting mess on cold days.

Your nose does more than just hold your glasses up; part of its function is to hydrate and warm incoming air, to protect your tender lungs from the cold, dry air in the atmosphere.

The colder the air, the harder your beak has to work to accomplish this miracle. Cold sensors high in the nasopharynx detect the cold air and direct more blood to its array of blood vessels. This both warms the air—and stimulates the mucous membranes to secrete more, which helps moisten the air you breathe.

You got it? Your nose runs because it's hard at work protecting your delicate lungs. If you don't like it, stay inside.

❋

米

Who Is a Jew, and Where the Heck Is He or She?

A Mishmash of Figures About Jews

Q *How many Jews are there in Madagascar, and what are their names?*

A Their names? Answering that part of your question is the moral equivalent of writing "I will not talk without raising my hand" 500 times on the blackboard.

Recently, Sol heard a story about Madagascar. Back in the 1950s, a follower of the Lubavitcher rebbe was planning a trip to Africa. Before the trip, the traveler visited the rebbe, who is legendary for never letting good opportunities go to waste—especially opportunities to make contact with new groups of Jews.

The traveler listed the three countries he was planning to visit. "Is that all?" the rebbe queried. The traveler listed the same three. "Is that *all?*" the rebbe asked again. And again, the same answer.

So the fellow left, and because of mechanical problems, the airplane landed in—you guessed it—Madagascar. The traveler realized that there had been a purpose in the rebbe's questions. He considered the issue carefully, and decided the rebbe wanted him to go out and find Jews in that remote corner of the world.

He did, and found six Jewish families.

All of which is a roundabout way of getting to your question, bubbe. While nobody seems to have an exact count of the Jewish population of that tiny nation off the southeast coast of Africa, the American Jewish Committee, which keeps track of such things, puts it in the "under fifty Jews" category. So if you're looking for a good corned beef on rye, don't shlep all the way to Madagascar.

Q *Are there any Jews in Antarctica?*

A Jews are many things, but as a group they're not stupid, which explains why warm Miami Beach and Tel Aviv are still popular watering holes for Jews, but Antarctica has never had much attraction for the bagel-eating set.

In case you haven't noticed, Antarctica has few permanent residents, at least of the human species. There have been numerous Jews manning scientific and military outposts, but as yet, no condos or decent delis.

The most southerly habitat for Jews is New Zealand—and there aren't many of them there. According to the American Jewish Committee's 1989 statistics, some 4,000 Jews call New Zealand home, along with the overabundance of sheep.

Q *Sol, do you have any knowledge at all about how many Jews in this country keep kosher?*

A Your question, buttercup, is a little like asking how many Americans pay every last cent of their tax obligations. There are figures, and then there are figures.

First, let's begin with the obvious fact that accurate statistics on such things are scarce, since the Kosher Police have yet to make their appearance on the American scene.

Also, there are many variations in "keeping kosher." Many people are strict in their observance. But how do you classify people who keep kosher at home, but fudge a little when they go to restaurants?

Several recent estimates—including polling data reported in *The New York Times*—put the number of "kosher consumers" at about six million. But don't get excited; some 4 million of those are members of other religions with similar dietary restrictions, including Muslims.

A survey cited in a recent *American Jewish Year Book* shows some regional differences; 36 percent of Jewish New Yorkers surveyed buy only kosher meat, but only 24 percent of Jewish Baltimorans—and a paltry 19 percent of Jews in St. Louis. Some of this is undoubtedly related to the higher concentration of Orthodox Jews in New York. But the figure also reflects the fact that kosher products are more readily available in big Eastern cities; in parts of Brooklyn, kosher butchers are as plentiful as taverns in Milwaukee.

The same study showed sharp decreases in the observance of the dietary laws. In Baltimore, for instance, the recent 24-percent figure represented a drop from 36 percent in 1965.

The two million Jews who buy and use kosher products represent about a third of the total Jewish population.

Q *Sol, how many people in this country currently know and use Yiddish? It seems to me that there has been something of a renaissance.*

A Most experts agree that there has been a resurgence in interest in Yiddish in recent years. Unfortunately, there are few statistics that speak to the issue one way or another.

The most recent statistics go all the way back to 1971, according to the folks at the YIVO Institute for Jewish

Research. Back then, it was estimated that more than two million Americans understood Yiddish, and a few hundred thousand less than that could speak it.

But only 757,000 or so could read Yiddish, and a paltry 566,000 could actually write the language.

Since then, it's anybody's guess about the prevalence of Yiddish. Older immigrants, for whom Yiddish was a primary language, are succumbing to old age. On the other hand, many post–Second World War arrivals from Eastern Europe continue to speak Yiddish—and these are groups that are reproducing at a tremendous rate.

Q *Why are there so few Jewish osteopaths? Is there something in Jewish law that would keep Jews from going into the profession—or from seeking care from an osteopath?*

A Sol posed your question to Dr. Binyamin Rothstein, who just about choked at your assertion that Jews shun osteopathy.

Rothstein is both an observant Jew and an osteopath, and an excellent advertisement for his profession.

According to Rothstein, a substantial proportion of his peers during his medical education were Jews; the president of the school, which happened to be in Des Moines, Iowa, was a rabbi.

So much for no Jews in osteopathy.

Osteopathy, the doctor said, takes a more holistic approach to our battered bodies than traditional medicine. The emphasis is on helping the body cure itself—and on various muscular-skeletal manipulations that are supposed to induce health.

Your basic internist would treat a sinus infection with an antibiotic, Rothstein said. So would an osteopath, but with the addition of manipulations to promote drainage.

Osteopaths, Rothstein said, operate under the principle of "find it, fix it, and get out of the way," which sounds okay to Sol.

And osteopathy, Rothstein said, is particularly compatible with Jewish law. "In fact, the Rambam talks about manipulations," he said. "It's a very appropriate way of treating the body."

Sol wonders what Dr. Rothstein could do with writer's cramp.

✳

Q *Why are there so few Jewish airline pilots?*

A Although there are no precise statistics on how many Jews are flying the friendly skies, your observation about the paucity of Jews in the cockpit was confirmed by several experts in the airline industry.

The reasons? Mostly, it has to do with where the airlines find pilots in the first place.

A high proportion of airline pilots are former military fliers, a fact that gives the airlines a substantial pool of trained and experienced pilots. And most military pilots are career officers, a group in which Jews have traditionally been underrepresented.

There are a number of reasons for this phenomenon. Few Jews seek military careers, in part because of traditional biases against Jews in the higher echelons of the armed services, in part because Jews have developed alternative paths to upward mobility.

Interestingly, airlines have been forced of late to look for pilots with nonmilitary backgrounds. There hasn't been a serious war for more than a decade and a half, thereby draining the reservoir pool of trained pilots waiting to be plucked up by the airlines. What this means for the future of Jewish pilots, Sol does not know.

But it may be true that Jews nowadays are more interested in *buying* airlines than flying for them.

✳

Q *Okay, Solly, it's almost election time, and everyone's talking about the Jewish vote. So tell me: do a greater proportion of Jews vote than non-Jews? I've always suspected that Jews are more community spirited than other people, so don't disillusion me.*

A Sol hates to throw cold water in your borscht, bubbe, but the bald facts about Jewish voting are not the kind of thing to set George Washington's heart throbbing.

While there are no exact figures, political scientists rank Jewish participation in presidential elections at maybe eight to ten percentage points higher than the national average.

While this may sound patriotic, remember that the national average is a dismal 50 percent. So maybe 6 in 10 Jews will turn out in your average presidential contest—good, but not exactly a living advertisement for democracy.

Q *What percentage of American Jews have been to Israel?*

A The subjective answer to your question is that *everyone* has been to Israel, except for Sol, who hasn't been able to figure out yet how to finagle one of those free trips for reporters.

Seriously, this is a touchy question for the authorities in Jerusalem, who estimate that a measly 15 percent of American Jews have made the trip. Of that number, of course, many have made the trip repeatedly.

Interestingly, only 40 percent of all American visitors to Israel are Jewish—down significantly in recent years. Israeli officials are somewhat mystified by this change. In part, they think, it's due to the growing interest in Israel as a fulfillment of prophecy for Christian groups. And during periods of disorder in Israel, they report, Jewish tourism drops off faster than Christian tourism.

Q *We keep hearing about a "birth dearth" in the Jewish community. Yet in New York, I see these huge Jewish families; you'd think they were 'Catholics. What gives?*

A As you so astutely observe, there is no birth dearth among the Orthodox, to whom reproduction is both a religious commandment and a social imperative.

But the Orthodox are a minority in the American Jewish world; the very Orthodox, who are procreating at the fastest clip, are a minority within this minority.

In Reform and Conservative circles, fertility rates more closely approximate the overall American averages. And, to put it plainly, those averages are below the replacement level.

A study a few years back by the National Opinion Research Center showed that the Jewish population is suffering the greatest net loss of any major religious group—a result of low birth rates, high rates of "never-married" singles, and the fact that more Jews are intermarrying, and fewer of their non-Jewish partners are converting to Judaism. Various Christian denominations have similar problems. But they have one big advantage over the Jews; many of them proselytize like all get out. So they have a steady influx of new members; Jews, who eschew that sort of thing, are not able to offset the attrition.

꙳

Q *Dear Sol: Who is a Jew?*

A Sol thought you people would *never* ask. After all, this question has been debated for centuries, the best minds in Judaism are still deadlocked, and the entire nation of Israel has been divided by the issue. And you want Sol the Answer Man to solve the problem once and for all in a newspaper column? No sweat.

Sol, a trusted friend to Orthodox, Reform, and everything in between, personally likes the way David Ben-Gurion allegedly solved this vexing problem. "Anyone meshuga enough to call himself a Jew *is* a Jew," Ben-Gurion said.

No doubt this will not appeal to those seeking some measure of theological purity. But if it's good enough for Ben-Gurion, it's good enough for Sol.

The Jewish Family and the Family of Jews

Jewish Family Life, Jewish Denominational Life

Q *If your great-grandmother was Jewish, or your grand-mother was Jewish, but your grandfather and great-grandfather were Methodist, does that mean you're still a Jew? Do only other Jews consider you Jewish, or do non-Jews consider you Jewish? Is it like being black in South Africa—one-tenth black, and you're all black?*

A If B'nai B'rith decided to give a Confused Jew of the Year award, you'd be a shoo-in, friend.

From a purely technical point of view, what matters is what your mother is. If *she's* Jewish, and if you haven't done something foolish like convert, you are Jewish, even if you don't know a shul from a White Castle hamburger joint.

So if your paternal grandmother was Methodist, but your maternal one Jewish, and no conversions intervened, you'd be Jewish. You could come from a long line of Methodists, descended from John Wesley himself, and still you'd be considered Jewish if your dad scandalized his family by picking a Jewish wife.

As for how the non-Jewish world classifies people of mixed heritage, this is more a matter of ephemeral fashion and raw prejudice than anything else. Christian law, for example, says that anyone who professes a belief in Christianity is a Christian. But in practice, the Christian masses have periodically viewed Jews more as a racial group or a tribe than as adherents of a very old religion.

This confusion among the gentiles is hardly surprising, since most American Jews are themselves hopelessly bewildered about whether they are part of a religion, a subculture, or a race.

※

Q *Why can't Jewish mothers leave their unmarried children alone? I mean, Sol, you'd think it was the greatest tragedy since the destruction of the Temple that I don't have a spouse yet, and I'm just pushing 30. Why is this?*

A First, let's cool the hysteria and try to sort things out a little. While precise statistics in this area are sparse, anecdotal evidence suggests that most mothers, Jewish and gentile, experience a certain anxiety when their adult children resist the lures of matrimony.

This undoubtedly springs from the universal idea of grandparenting as revenge; there's nothing sweeter than having your ungrateful adult children deal with little ingrates of their very own.

That being said, Jewish law and tradition are filled with injunctions favoring marriage and family, and deploring the single state. "Be fruitful and multiply" isn't referring to agriculture, bubbe; it means you, a fact that your shrewd mom is not likely to miss.

Moreover, Jews have traditionally been driven by a certain demographic imperative to reproduce. Throughout the ages,

Jewish survival has depended upon keeping up the birth rate. Judaism, too, is a home-centered religion, with a strong emphasis on children.

Sol's advice? Get yourself a spouse and quit your kvetching.

✳

Q *Sol, your advice to a single pushing 30 about the parental, not to mention societal, pressure to get married, is to "get yourself a spouse and quit your kvetching."*

For people attracted to the opposite sex, this advice is bad enough; for people attracted to individuals of the same sex it is unbearable.

A Well, perhaps Sol was a little quick on the trigger with that answer. Sol is well aware of the many single Jews of various sexual orientations for whom the quest for companionship is a very real and serious problem.

But the fact remains that we are talking about a religious tradition that puts a strong emphasis on marriage and family. No doubt this puts a certain pressure on those who have not entered into such arrangements—gay, straight, and celibate.

Sol, being a mere Answer Man without even a shred of rabbinic training, has no intention of making pronouncements about homosexuality. The different branches of Judaism treat homosexuality with varying degrees of tolerance.

It is legitimate to hope that the Jewish community will learn to treat its homosexual component with sensitivity; it is not realistic to imagine that Jewish parents will stop hoping for marriage, children, and—ultimate bliss—medical degrees.

✳

Q *I assume there is some Biblical or Talmudic reason Jews don't name their kids after living relatives, but for the* *life of me I can't figure out what it is. Enlighten us, O Wise One.*

A Sol modestly thanks you for the well-deserved compliment; you are indeed a person of discernment.

But not much: all Jews don't observe this custom, just Ashkenazic Jews. Although the origins of this custom are somewhat unclear, it is probably related to the idea that naming a child after old Uncle Pinchas might just somehow cut down on the days remaining to the geezer.

Ashkenazim *do* name their children after particularly admired but deceased relatives, although in the transition from the Old Country culture to modern America, the names are often mauled beyond recognition.

Among the Sephardim, on the other hand, naming children after living relatives is not a no-no. In fact, it's considered prudent to name a new kid after a relative who might serve as a particularly good role model. But generally not the father; even among the Sephardim, you're not likely to find many "Juniors" running around the playlot.

⁂

Q *Is it better for a pious woman to marry a good Christian or an evil Jew?*

A What's this, someone's holding a gun to her head? Are you suggesting that this poor pious woman has only these two choices?

If it sounds like Sol is dodging your question, you're right; rabbis get paid for this kind of thinking, and even many of them would give you a similar answer.

Obviously, we're not cutting any new furrows here by suggesting that the traditional prohibitions against intermarriage are still deeply embedded in Jewish life—though you'd scarcely know it, if you look at a cross section of American Jewry.

No rabbi of Sol's acquaintance actually condones intermarriage; few, even from the Reform camp, will officiate at marriages between Jews and non-Jews without conversion of the non-Jewish partner.

On the Orthodox end of the spectrum, the answer is a little more resounding; for them, it is purely a matter of Torah. If you don't like this Jew, they'd probably counsel, you have no choice but to find another one.

And if another is not available ... well, many Orthodox rabbis would tell you, an evil Jew is preferable to a nice, cuddly non-Jew, although they would be quick to point out the improbability of such a dilemma.

If this sounds tough as nails, it is; these Torah-true Jews don't take prisoners when it comes to the basic commandments that have traditionally regulated Jewish life.

✳

Q *Sol, a lot of people in my circle are into breast-feeding their children. Is this okay, in terms of Jewish tradition? Does Judaism have anything to say about breast-feeding a child for an extended period?*

A Sol is a little astounded by your question. Do you honestly think the Matriarchs ran down to the 7-Eleven for formula every time their kids got hungry?

In Jewish tradition, breast-feeding occupies a place of honor right up there with breathing; until fairly recently, it wasn't even an option for mothers and their offspring.

Of course, Orthodox Jews also value modesty, so most rabbis would undoubtedly counsel discretion when little Schlomo chows down.

As for extended periods of nursing, what did you have in mind? Kindergarten? Junior high? Were you planning on accompanying the little guy to college so he could avoid the horrors of weaning?

Sol is advised that Jewish tradition does not frown on extended breast-feeding, as long as you don't go overboard. In the Talmud, two years is considered acceptable. Moderation is the key; to decide exactly what is moderate, Sol suggests a good, long talk with your rabbi.

✳

Q *What are the most popular names for Jewish children these days? Are some lesser-known Biblical names making a comeback?*

A According to several of Sol's rabbinic advisers, who are at the cutting edge of such things, Biblical names continue their comeback—with some new trends, and, of course, a lot of regional variations. Trends in baby names in the Jewish citadel of New York are obviously different from trends among the 350-member Jewish community of Tuscaloosa, Alabama, for instance.

With that cautionary note, let us proceed. According to these observers, Sarah, Rebecca, and Rachel are the current Big Three for girls; on the male side of the ledger, Benjamin and Adam appear to be clear winners, along with the ever-popular Alexander—not exactly a name with good associations in Jewish history.

Other biggies include Nathan, Jesse, Leah, Noah, Jonathan, and Jacob.

A few years ago, one rabbi reports, Jews veered off the 10-year-old Biblical naming kick into upper-crust WASP names, like Ashleigh and Courtney—thus giving rise to such unusual constructions as "Ashleigh Slutsky."

But the Biblical names have made a big comeback. So have some names that, until recently, have been associated primarily with grandparents; according to several observers, there are a growing number of ankle-biters with names like Max and Sophie.

※

Q *Can you tell me what cities have the highest rates of intermarriage?*

A This is one of those wonderful examples of how statistics almost make sense, if you think about them long enough.

Consider your question logically: where would Jewish young people be most likely to meet and marry members of other religions? Probably not in Borough Park in Brooklyn, where there are more Jews per capita than just about any place except Tel Aviv. But it's a different story in smaller cities, away from the major Jewish population centers.

The statistics verify this guess. The highest intermarriage rates occur in the West, about as far from New York, Philadelphia, and Baltimore as you can get.

Intermarriage, researchers have found, is most directly related to the size of the Jewish marriage market. Yes, they actually get paid for coming to such astonishing conclusions.

Paradoxically, some of these smaller Western cities show the highest rates of synagogue affiliation among Jews—but also the highest rates of intermarriage. The residents of these areas may feel Jewish, but when it comes to romance, the market is just too sparse.

Q *I know this is a stupid question, Sol, but can a religious Jewish divorce be used in lieu of a civil divorce? I was thinking maybe it would be cheaper than all those lawyers and things.*

A Think again, friend. You're going to be disappointed on several counts.

First a *get*—an official Jewish religious divorce—is not accepted by the secular authorities anywhere but Israel. If you're a Conservative or an Orthodox Jew and you're about to go splitsville, you'll need both a *get* and a civil divorce. Reform Judaism has pretty much done away with any need for the *get*.

As for the *get* being cheaper, you may be in for a shock. Religious divorces are still done the old way—by scribes, in Aramaic. It can cost upwards of $150 or $250 to pay for the scribe, the rabbis, and the incidentals.

Q *Why does Judaism have this thing about matrilineal descent? I mean, what difference does it make whether it's your mom or your dad who is Jewish?*

A The short answer is that it's in the Talmud, bubbe, which is good enough for most Orthodox people.

Those on the Reform end of the spectrum take a more historical approach. Matrilineal descent, they suggest, was a practical adaptation in a more tribal time, when determining one's parentage was a matter of major importance.

Now think about it: determining the *mother* of a new baby is the simplest thing in the world, but determining the *father* may require, shall we say, a leap of faith.

So the Jews, being intensely practical people, fixed on mom as the bearer of the Jewish heritage, a position that is still supported by Orthodox and Conservative Jews.

To Reform Jews, this idea no longer serves the needs of the Jewish community, especially not in an era of assimilation and intermarriage. To them, it makes more sense in this day and age to accept you as a full-fledged Jew if either your mother or your father was Jewish—a position, they say, that will help keep many children of intermarriage within the Jewish community.

⌖

Q *Sol, I was wondering about the question of alimony and child support in Jewish law. When a woman gets a get, does Jewish law have an equivalent of alimony or child support?*

A An interesting question. In Orthodox marriage contracts, there are generally provisions built in providing for alimony, in the event that wedded bliss decides to take a holiday.

But alas, these provisions usually provide for only symbolic payments, not even enough money to buy a bus ticket to Miami.

Among Sephardim, it is customary to negotiate alimony at

the time of the marriage, a tradition that looks suspiciously like foresight, in view of today's 50-percent divorce rate.

As for child support, a parent's responsibility to a child is clearly specified in *Halachah*—a somewhat different obligation for boy and girl children. Girls must be supported until the time of their marriage, while boys require parental support only until they are capable of entering the work force.

Of course, the rabbis who wrote these rules had in mind a somewhat different social climate, when boys went to work around the time they became a bar mitzvah, not after four years of college, six of graduate school, and a few extra years to "find themselves."

※

Q *Do people still have "Levirate" marriages? And while you're at it, why don't you explain what a Levirate marriage is? Is it anything like a leveraged buy out?*

A Let's do this by example. Say you marry Mitzi, and then immediately have the chutzpah to die and leave the poor gal a widow.

In the old days, your brother then would have been required to marry Mitzi so your good name could be carried on—the "levir's duty" referred to in Deuteronomy 25:5.

If your brother declined the honor, he would have to go through the *halitzah* ceremony, in which the shmegegge is officially chastised for not fulfilling his obligation.

There are some problems with this whole idea, not the least of which is that your brother may already have a spouse. Polygamy was acceptable in Biblical days—Solomon, according to legend, had between 700 and 1,000 wives, depending on how one defines a wife. But the practice was pretty much outlawed in Judaism sometime around the year 1000, although some Sephardic groups retained it until fairly recently.

Another problem with Levirate marriages is that while the practice is described in the Book of Deuteronomy, another

section of the Bible—Leviticus—insists that a marriage between a woman and her brother-in-law is incest.

So in modern times, Orthodox Jews have retained only one
part of the practice—the *halitzah* ceremony. Conservatives
prefer to ignore the whole question, and Reform Jews have
officially plucked the entire idea of Levirate marriage from
their theology.

The icing on the cake is that Levirate marriages are
prohibited in Israel.

⁂

Q *Why aren't observant Jews called "conservative," since
that's what they are, in a theological sense? And Conservative
Jews maybe ought to be called "middle of the roaders"?*

A When you get into the realm of religious labels, bubbe,
you enter treacherous waters indeed. One man's orthodoxy is
another's heresy, and so on.

In the case of Conservative Judaism, it's all a question of
relativity.

Conservative Judaism arose sometime around the midpoint
of the last century as an offshoot of a Reform movement that
was changing the rules for many Jews. In Europe it was
known primarily as "Historical Judaism."

Like the Reform movement, Historical Judaism favored
the integration of Jews into modern Western society. Unlike
their Reform-minded colleagues, they did not promote a
wholesale rejection of ritual. The Conservatives, for instance,
favored retention of the laws of *kashrut;* even in the early
days, the Reform movement was apparently preparing itself
for today's fast-food culture.

So compared to the Reform movement from whence it
sprang, Conservative Judaism is, indeed, conservative. As for
the Orthodox, many of them resent any implication that
they are "conservative," because to them, their beliefs and
practices represent the unchanging core of the Jewish
tradition.

Q *What is a Reconstructionist Jew? When I was a kid, there were Reform, Conservative, and Orthodox—period. Now I hear about this other business. Is it new?*

A Where have you spent your life, on the moon? Kansas City? Like so many other religious questions, the definition of Reconstructionism depends on your perspective. Some have called the movement the "conscience" of the Jewish world. Others regard it as a terrific religion for atheists.

The bare facts are these: the movement was formed in the early part of this century by Rabbi Mordecai Kaplan, who emphasized the cultural and ethnic aspects of Jewish life, not the traditional religious ones.

In terms of religious expression, Kaplan used a pick-and-choose approach. He rejected the notion of the Jews as the "Chosen People," but retained a core of observances that, in his theology, reflected the highest values of the Jewish people. He also discarded the idea of a transcendent deity, preferring a more naturalistic divine being. In some ways, the movement presaged today's "Jewish Humanist" groups.

The reason you never heard of it is that Reconstructionism has not yet overwhelmed the Jewish establishment. According to some estimates, there are only 7,000 Reconstructionists, most of whom live in the New York area, which may well need more reconstruction than most regions of the country.

On the other hand, a number of other cities report increasing activity by Reconstructionists in recent years.

Q *How come there are no Jews named Wayne or Duane?*

A Is this a representative sample of how you exercise your brain? Of all the mysteries of modern Jewish life, is this the one troubling you the most? Please excuse Sol while he emits a long sigh.

First, disabuse yourself of the notion that in the entire

Jewish world, there is not a single Wayne or Duane. Several of Sol's top advisers revealed the dirty little secret that they have known Jewish Waynes and Duanes, although they conceded that these are not on the American Jewish Hit Parade of Names.

But hey, if you searched hard enough, you could probably find Jews named Christian, or Abdul. Wayne and Duane are a piece of cake, relatively speaking.

There is no single reason for the paucity of Jewish Waynes and Duanes. Neither name harks back to a Father of the Church or a pagan god. Wayne is an Old English name, derived from "wainright"—a guy who fixes wagons. Duane comes from the Gallic; it means something like "dark-complected."

But there are discernible subcultural fashions in our society when it comes to names. There are proportionally more Benjamins and Nathans crawling around Jewish nurseries than Waynes and Duanes, or Beaus, or Christophers, or Theresas.

In the American Jewish community, names from other traditions often become popular. But generally, these are names that have already caught on with the non-Jewish elites, or names that have rocketed to prominence because of popular television shows or celebrities.

Wayne and Duane have never been wildly popular in the broader culture; as a result, they have not crossed the line into the Jewish community in a major way.

TEN

"I Fought the Law and the Law Won"

A Highly Cursory Cruise Through Jewish Law

Q *When do you light Shabbat candles if you live in the Land of the Midnight Sun?*

A Sheeesh, the questions you people ask.

You use a clock, bubbe. To be precise, you—or the local rabbinic authorities, not that any rabbinic authority with a lick of sense would live in an igloo—work out a schedule based on twelve hours of theoretical light, twelve of theoretical darkness.

If, on the other hand, you live in Leningrad, where summer nights don't offer enough darkness to get mugged by, you rely on local rabbis who make calculations about the time of the lowest placement of the sun, and work backwards from there. And if you live in the British Empire, diminished though it may be, you rely on the national rabbinate in Scotland, who have long provided an international standard for candle-

lighting time in regions of the world where the sun does weird things.

In case you're interested, such questions have been the topic of lively halachic debate, along with this one: what would an observant Jewish astronaut do? Think about it: if you were orbiting the earth on a Friday, candle-lighting time would come every hour or so.

Fortunately, there's a halachic answer for that, as well; for airborne or spaceborne travelers, candle-lighting time is determined by the appropriate time at the point of departure.

And if you really wanted to ask a creative question, you could have asked what Jews would do on the moon. Here on earth, Jewish observances are based on the moon's gyrations from the perspective of our home planet.

Believe it or not, the Israeli military rabbinate held a session a few years back to discuss this very problem. Basically, they came up with the same answer; Shabbat starts for Jewish tourists on the moon at the same earth time as it would start at their point of origin—Cape Canaveral, no doubt, since until recently, the Soviets have tended to fling their Jews into jail, not space.

Since a "day" on the moon is the equivalent of 14 earth days, earthlings on that forsaken chunk of rock would celebrate the Sabbath twice for each lunar day—in case anybody's interested, which Sol seriously doubts.

Q *Sol, if you're bald, and you wear a rug, is that considered a head-cover or must you still wear a yarmulke? And speaking of rugs, does Michael Milken wear a rug?*

A Although it's true that one rarely sees boxes of loaner toupees at the entrances to sanctuaries, wigs are, in fact, considered to be roughly the equivalent of yarmulkes, as far as most Orthodox authorities are concerned.

Interestingly, the matter of toupees, like so many other fine points of Jewish law in a modern world, remains a lively topic of debate in halachic circles. Does the law apply only to

Loaner Toupees

toupees, for example, or would it also apply to, say, a "hair weave"? What about hair transplants?

From a purely practical point of view, most people wear rugs because they're self-conscious about their glistening pates; entering an Orthodox synagogue with only a toupee would be a dead giveaway to one's tonsorial infirmity.

As for Mr. Milken, he has enough problems without Sol commenting on his hairstyle.

⁂

Q *Can Jews be excommunicated?*

A If you're planning on doing something kinky, Sol's advice is, don't do it. Chances are you won't get excommunicated—that's a remedy that has been applied sparingly in recent centuries—but there are plenty of other penalties in this world.

The idea of *herem* goes way back in Jewish tradition. In the old days, there were different degrees of excommunication, ranging from a kind of seven-day voluntary exile for such offenses as insulting a scholar, to actual banishment from the community.

Sometimes, threats of *herem* were used for shady purposes, including fund-raising. This practice has not been adopted by modern Jewish fund-raising organizations, all appearances notwithstanding.

Probably the most famous excommunication in Jewish history was that of Baruch Spinoza, the Portuguese-Dutch philosopher who was given the heave-ho in 1656 for his heretical views. The elders of the community didn't mince words: "May he be cursed in the day and cursed in the night, cursed in his lying down and cursed in his rising up," they wrote in their sentence.

And the Vilna Gaon—his name was Rabbi Elijah ben Solomon Zalman, and his title reflected his stature as a scholar—placed the entire Chasidic movement in *herem* in 1772, the ultimate step in the battle between the Chasidim and Mitnaggedim. The ban was a miserable failure, as today's thriving Lubavitcher community suggests.

The problem with excommunication in Judaism also points to one of our greatest strengths: the lack of central authority, and the wide variety of views co-existing under the Jewish umbrella. It's hard enough to get a bunch of Jews to agree on, say, the basic qualities that make one a Jew, much less the finer points of religious doctrine.

Q *Why don't rabbis wear digital watches?*

A Funny you should ask: at a recent meeting of rabbis, Sol was struck by the fact that not one out of almost 90 rabbis wore a digital watch.

Like so many questions of ancient law applied to modern circumstances, the answer is not entirely clear. In fact, there appears to be nothing in Jewish law that actually prohibits the wearing of a high-tech Casio. But the matter of digital watches on Shabbat has been the subject of a good deal of rabbinic give-and-take in recent years; a digital watch is, after all, an electrical instrument, the same as a light bulb or a dishwasher.

But is a digital watch passive? After all, it's not necessary to the watch's operation that you actually *do* anything except look at it. Or is the wearing of the watch tantamount to operating it?

This is just a hint of the debate that has gone on in halachic circles for quite some time. Sol's own theory goes like this: most rabbis generally get their watches as awards at various banquets, and who'd be tacky enough to award a digital watch to a religious leader?

Q *A lot of Christians these days talk about the apocalypse and Armageddon and things. I'm wondering: in Jewish teaching about the coming of the Messiah, what happens to non-Jews?*

A Interestingly, Jewish messianism is a lot kinder to non-believers than Christian millennialism, which predicts a hot and unhappy future for the "unsaved."

Judaism teaches that non-Jews have a perfectly respectable place in God's scheme. Maimonides taught that non-Jews only have to obey the seven "Noachide" laws that comprise the basis of all civilization in order to earn a portion of the world to come. These are the real basics, like prohibitions against murder, theft, and blasphemy.

Jews, on the other hand, are required to observe all 613 *mitzvoth* assigned specifically to the Chosen People.

Hey, did Sol say it was supposed to be easy?

Q *What do observant Jews do when they get a haircut? Is it permissible to take their head coverings off? And what is the origin of the requirement to keep one's head covered, and why are there so many variations in its practice?*

A My, we are curious today. Sol has never observed that Orthodox Jews are dumb; when they visit the barber or take a shower, they do what any sensible person would do—they doff their headgear.

As for the origins of the practice of covering the noggin, the answers are a little unclear. Some scholars insist that keeping one's head covered at all times dates back to the days of Moses, although only high priests were specifically directed to do this. Others insist that the custom originated in Talmudic times, when scholars and men of learning kept their pates covered.

No kidding, this is not a simple halachic issue. For ages, scholars have debated the real function of a head cover. Is it intended as a symbol of observance? As a sign of the fear of God? As a practical form of apparel?

The exact *type* of hat worn by Orthodox Jews is mostly a matter of local custom. Some people believe that the more "traditional" the Jew, the larger the head covering. Jews with a more Kabbalistic orientation often wear two head coverings; Chasids often wear a yarmulke under the traditional brimmed hat.

Note to Readers:

In a recent column, Sol impetuously tackled the issue of why Jews cover their heads in synagogue, and variations in the practice among different groups of Jews.

Not surprisingly, Sol's somewhat flip answer provoked a barrage of letters that demonstrates once again that Jews are a diverse and outspoken bunch.

One of the most outspoken missives came from Herbert Schwartz, professor emeritus of something or other at New York University, who offers a lucid, if lengthy account of the head-covering controversy. Professor Schwartz's letter, edited somewhat for space, follows.

Sol, no kidding, this *is* a simple halachic issue. However, it does involve a complex social situation, which will probably never be laid to rest as long as there are Jews with heads to be covered.

This "issue" is a fine example of custom assuming, and

even usurping, the force of law. There is, in fact, no law on this matter; the Talmud is quite specific in restricting head coverings to men who are endowed with certain responsibilities in the community, such as judges, priests, etc., and to married women.

Even as custom, it seems to have arisen fairly recently in the long history of the Jewish people, since in the thirteenth century Rabbi Isaac of Vienna wrote of his disapproval of the then-prevailing practice of rabbis reciting blessings with heads uncovered. As late as the seventeenth century Rabbi David Ha-Levi of Ostrog was arguing that Jews at prayer ought to cover heads if only because Christians do not do so.

What is engaging about this whole matter is that it continues to persist despite the effort of the sixteenth century's great Talmudist, Rabbi Solomon Luria, whose famous responsum (#72) should have put an end to the whole matter. In it, he not only insisted that he knew of no prohibition against praying with uncovered head, he cited Tractate Soferim to support the notion that even the Shema may be recited in public with uncovered head.

Professor Schwartz went on in this scholarly vein, but you readers with short attention spans get the idea; the requirement of covered pates has been a subject of lively debate over the centuries, and will probably be settled once and for all about the time we answer questions like "Which color is better, red, or green?"

The good professor seems to have a good grasp of the endlessness of this debate: "Of course, Sol, even this response of mine to your article won't really affect the matter in the slightest, will it?" he writes. "But, it gives me as much fun to respond as it seems to have given you to have said what you did!"

Professor Schwartz is a real live wire, and Sol thanks him for the info.

Q *Why do we call "sideburns" sideburns? Do sideburns, if left to grow, become the sidecurls you see on Orthodox Jews? And why don't Orthodox Jews shave?*

A Do you often have trouble focusing on a single subject, bubbe? Or is this your idea of a wide-ranging intellectual pursuit?

"Sideburns" arise from a linguistic mixup; the clumps of hair along the rim of the face refer to a Civil War general by the name of Burnsides who sported that particular style of side whiskers. Somewhere in the mist of history, people became confused and began calling them "sideburns."

As to your other question, Orthodox Jews don't all sport beards or wear sidecurls, as you may have noticed. But many strictly Orthodox Jews observe this Biblical injunction: "You shall not round the corners of your heads, neither shall you destroy the corners of your beard."

Pruning the sideburns would violate the prohibition against rounding the corners of the head; shaving would obviously destroy the corners of the beard.

There are a variety of viewpoints about these prohibitions, of course. Some rabbis have maintained that pruning a beard with scissors is acceptable, since it can't cut the hair off flush with the skin. Other rabbis have maintained that electric razors likewise do not cut close enough to trigger the injunction against shaving.

But then along came Victor Kiam, and now there is active discussion in rabbinic circles about whether the new generation of electric razors crosses the line, so to speak.

❋

Q *If a nuclear attack is imminent on Shabbat, may an observant Jew drive out of town?*

A Sure he can, but a fat lot of good it will do him: with the urban interstates turning into parking lots and stoplights multiplying like rabbits on special fertility hormones, he'd probably do just as well climbing into his basement and covering himself with an old mattress, as one 1950s Civil Defense manual suggested in describing how to survive a nuclear attack.

Jewish law is replete with the idea that laws like those governing the Sabbath can be suspended when lives are at stake. If you have a heart attack on Saturday, no sane rabbi would suggest you postpone the ambulance ride until Sunday; if you have a medical condition that prohibits fasting, nobody would suggest that you jeopardize your health by going without food.

The same goes for nuclear attack—although, in the case of incoming ICBMs, prayer might be as efficacious as flight.

Q *Can an observant Jew work at the* National Enquirer?
A Sol posed your question to a rabbi of his acquaintance, a man not known for an overabundance of humor. "Of course he could, if he held his nose very tightly," said this rabbi, emitting a little chortle. But then, being a rabbi, he quickly grew serious and delivered an opinion.

To wit: it would be hard to work for a newspaper that writes about two-headed space monsters and the sexual habits of the rich and famous without violating a slew of commandments—not the least of which are the injunctions against bearing false witness and spreading gossip.

Indeed, "evil speech" is one of the most discussed violations of Jewish law. He who tells or believes slander, the sages teach, deserves to be cast to the dogs and stoned.

Sol, of course, would never presume to judge the journalistic integrity of the *Enquirer,* which has foolishly chosen not to enhance its pages with this very column. Perhaps if Sol began investigating the possible extra-terrestrial infiltration of *yeshivot* in Flatbush . . .

Q *If a pious man gets a blood transfusion, does it matter if he receives blood from someone who does not observe the dietary laws?*

A Even if there was such a prohibition, it would not apply in cases of life and death. And in Sol's experience, very few blood transfusions are done for the pure joy of it.

But the argument doesn't need to go that far. What is different about a Jew is not biological . . . it's a matter of belief and observance.

To put it another way, Jews who keep kosher don't do so because eating *treife* will kill them; they do it in obedience to a commandment, and because obeying that commandment is part of their religious identity. Being tainted through transfusions from pork eaters is not much of a concern.

Q *Dear Sol: Could a Jew who keeps kosher play football, and therefore come into intimate contact with pigskin? Would such a person be forced to play a position like tackle, and not pick up fumbles even if they came to him?*

A This matter of pigs can get sort of ridiculous. Let's try this one more time: observant Jews aren't supposed to eat pigs. They can touch pigs, look at pigs, use products made from pigs, or put their money in wallets made with pigskin.

In the same way, a Jew can wear shoes made from the skin of cows killed in a non-kosher way, or wipe the bathroom counter with a real sponge—also a non-kosher animal, in case you get a craving for sponge. Hey, Jews can even go see *Jaws* at the movies, even though shark is a prohibited fish.

Get the idea? It's what you eat that's *treife*, not what you look at or touch.

Of course, if this hypothetical Orthodox Jew of yours played against the Chicago Bears, he might actually be forced to eat the ball, which would be a whole different problem.

Q *What if a pious man lends money to his temple and it defaults? Should he get a lawyer and sue?*

A What's your problem, you never heard of a rabbinical court? It's not exactly Judge Wapner, but the traditional *bet din,* consisting of three rabbis with a solid grounding in the myriad complexities of Jewish law, has been an effective way of resolving all kinds of business disputes between Jews. This goes back to the days when Jews could not count on the secular courts to provide a fair hearing.

Of course, both your friend and the synagogue would have to enter into the *bet din* process agreeing that its ruling would be binding. Incidentally, secular courts have repeatedly supported the judgments of rabbinical courts in this kind of dispute.

Of course, you could take such a complaint to the secular courts. But if you're Orthodox, you might find your circle of friends suddenly shrinking.

Is it right to pursue the debt? That, of course, is a matter of individual conscience. But one rabbi Sol consulted wisely said that a debt is a debt is a debt. Officials at your synagogue are not exempt from the legal or the moral responsibility to pay what they owe.

On the other hand, maybe you could forgive the debt; if you're lucky, they might name a folding chair after you.

Q *May a pious man work on a whaling ship?*

A Jews are a people of many occupations and professions, but Sol has never personally encountered a Jewish Captain Ahab. Generally, American Jews get their aquatic life at Sea World, not on the high seas.

This absence of Jewish whalers may be related to two factors—three, actually, if you count the fact that darned few Jews live anywhere near a whaling port.

First, whaling, to put it indelicately, is a particularly brutal and inhumane form of hunting. Ritual slaughter in Jewish life emphasizes the humane treatment of the animals involved; it's hard to imagine how a *shochet*—a ritual slaughterer—could perform humane slaughter on a gigantic, angry whale on the heaving sea.

It's a moot point, anyway, since whale meat is *treife;* it seems pretty silly to say it, but whales are mammals that don't chew their cuds or have cloven hooves. So Jews can't eat the stuff—not that there is a great lurking desire within the Jewish community for whale meat.

Can Jews *trade* in whale meat? One rabbi Sol consulted on this weighty matter was incredulous. "Why would they want to?" he asked.

Still, a direct involvement in commerce in forbidden foods is forbidden. So don't even think of buying that super new Whaleburger franchise.

Q *What does Jewish law say about income taxes? Could one make a good case that forking over to the IRS is against Jewish law?*

A Sure you could use that argument. And you'd have a lot of time to really perfect it—say 15 to 20 in Leavenworth.

The good news is that in times past, Jewish law has contributed to tax avoidance, and Sol is not talking tax shelters here. But the bad news is that this same body of law suggests that you should cough up your fair share to Uncle Sam and his cohorts in state and city treasuries.

The distinction is this: Jewish law mandates accepting civil law as you would Torah law—as long as the civil law does not conflict with Torah.

So in the Old Country, discriminatory taxes leveled just on Jews were regarded as illegitimate by the Jewish authorities; it was perfectly proper, at least from a Jewish point of view, to avoid such taxes.

Of course the local authorities saw it in a different light, which caused grief for a lot of Jews.

In this country, there's a general assumption that the tax system is reasonably fair ... stop choking, Sol said *reasonably*. There are no special tax burdens imposed on the Jewish population; there are no formal limitations on the economic activities of Jewish Americans.

It is the genius of America that everybody suffers the depredations of the IRS; there isn't a Jewish surtax, or a special 1040J form, the "J" standing for Jewish. Therefore, rabbinic authorities would suggest, the laws should be obeyed.

So if you want to observe Jewish law and at the same time keep your tuchis out of the slammer, pay up.

Interestingly, some of our Jewish forebears got in hot water with the American authorities because of their somewhat casual attitude toward taxes. After all, in the *shtetl*, they were accustomed to trying to outfox the tax collector. How were they to know that in this country, Jews were not singled out for special attention by the tax authorities?

🟥

Q *Any advice in Jewish law about finding a competent doctor or an honest auto mechanic?*

A No problem, at least as far as doctors are concerned. Find one with a good track record—specifically, one who has cured at least three different people.

Jewish law takes a somewhat different tack on this than, say, the American Medical Association. In our society, becoming a physician requires credentials; in Jewish tradition, it just requires a proven ability to heal people.

On one hand, this is an eminently practical approach; a lot of real *pishers* have somehow earned medical school diplomas.

But it also can give the Jewish stamp of approval on practitioners of more dubious disciplines; a lucky homeopathist, for example, might easily claim three cures out of a few thousand cases thanks to the laws of probability.

But the basic idea makes a lot of sense; forget all those physician referral services, and just find a doctor who can point to a good record.

An honest car mechanic? Sorry, bubbe, Jewish law doesn't waste much time dealing with the impossible.

※

Q *There are a lot of missionaries in my town, and some of them hand out Christian Bibles.*

Now some of my friends maintain that it's a mitzvah to take these Bibles and throw them in the next trash can as a way of disrupting their soul-saving activities.

But I wonder: our Scriptures are contained in their Bible. Wouldn't it be wrong to discard these words in some trash can?

A What are you, the Rambo of the anti-missionary world? Sol would bet that you're great fun at PTA meetings; some teacher criticizes *your* kid, and you'd probably sue for slander.

Sol posed your question to two rabbis, both of whom squirmed at what is obviously a delicate question of inter-group relations.

On the one hand, from a strictly technical point of view, a section of the Hebrew Scriptures incorporated into a Christian Bible is not treated as a sacred entity. The words may be the same, but the intent of the people who put it on paper in this particular form renders it qualitatively different from the genuine Jewish text.

The intent is what gives the written Torah holiness; the identical words, written in a Christian Bible, do not have the same quality to a Jew.

But as a practical matter, don't you think it's a little tacky to treat another person's religion in the same way that you'd treat a Big Mac wrapper—even if that person gave you the Bible because he was hustling your precious little soul?

Would you not consider it offensive if a person of another

religion treated your religious materials in a similar fashion?

Sol has always been a little mystified at the fear of missionaries within the Jewish community. Let's face it: generally speaking, these evangelists who "witness" on street corners are not firing on all six cylinders. Jewish losses to these folks are minimal, and probably not much higher than they'd be if Christianity had faded from the scene centuries ago. If it wasn't Christianity, there would be losses to Zen, or meditation, or one of those programs that let you exchange vast amounts of money for the privilege of learning better bladder control.

Get Sol's drift? If Judaism is a sound product, there's little to fear from the missionaries or their Bibles.

Q *My 16-year-old child wants to wear a single pierced earring. I am concerned, especially since this is a boy. What say the Jewish sages?*

A From a strictly non-halachic vantage point, Sol counsels you to be tolerant; in today's bizarre environment, a single earring is the least of your worries. Your kid could develop an unnatural interest in leather, or chopped motorcycles; he could sit around all day and watch reruns of "The Brady Bunch." He could become a *Republican,* for heaven's sake. Think of it.

The debate over earrings continues to be a lively one in Orthodox circles. Generally, the practice is accepted—don't jump all over Sol, there are obviously some rabbis who cite prohibitions against self-mutilation and unnecessary surgery in opposing ear-piercing, but this does not appear to be the norm.

A more important question involves the issue of . . . dare we say it? . . . cross dressing.

Jews are strictly forbidden to wear the apparel of the opposite sex. A Jewish man is forbidden to wear dresses, for instance, or dye his gray hair—a feminine practice, in the eyes of the rabbis of old. And they weren't even thinking of the Hellenizing influence of Grecian Formula.

But in practice, Jewish law takes some notice of local standards. Wearing a single pierced ear has become a fairly common practice among young men, a group naturally prone to such lapses of good taste. As such, many rabbis would no longer consider the single earring to be feminine—especially rabbis interested in outreach.

Now if your kid had in mind two earrings—big hoops, maybe, or crosses—the rabbis might well take a less tolerant stance toward your wayward adolescent.

Again, please don't take Sol's word for any of this; get ten rabbis in a room, and you'll end up with at least that many opinions on the poor boy with one pierced ear.

But rabbis, being practical souls, would also probably counsel patience. Adolescence, like most afflictions, passes without leaving lasting scars.

Q *Can a Jewish prostitute still join a synagogue? How about a mobster? A used-car salesman? What I'm getting at is this: can one's behavior in the outside world disqualify a person from the Jewish world?*

A Judaism, even in its strictest interpretations, is a surprisingly tolerant religion. So if you do something illegal, or merely stupid, your rabbi is not going to ride you out of town on a rail, unless you do something truly unforgivable, like becoming an Amway salesman.

Generally, there is nothing in Jewish law to bar such individuals from synagogue membership. Jews who sin remain Jews; there's always the hope that they will clean up their acts, and then maybe join the synagogue Brotherhood or Sisterhood.

But whether you want to give these miscreants synagogue honors is a different story. A mobster who does not mend his ways is unlikely to be called to the Torah. Nor would his financial contributions be particularly welcome, at least contributions derived from illicit activities.

An important point here is repentance; a repentant sinner is no longer a sinner, in the eyes of Jewish authorities. His dough is as good as anyone else's.

✳

Q *Sol, it would seem pretty obvious that Jewish law forbids suicide. But when you go to Israel, you're bombarded with the image of Masada and the martyrs who killed themselves when their capture seemed inevitable. Weren't they violating Jewish law?*

A As you suggest, Jewish law takes a dim view of suicide, to the extent that people who kill themselves are normally denied funeral and mourning rites. And suicides have no share in the world to come, according to Jewish teaching.

But the law is more lenient when it comes to certain categories of suicides, including suicides intended to keep the victim from committing the sins of murder, adultery, or idol worship.

In actual practice, Jewish tradition tends to distinguish between suicides who are in full possession of their wits, and those whose mental equilibrium is disturbed by particularly difficult circumstances. Let's face it: stable, happy people generally don't do themselves in. The application of Jewish law wisely recognizes this fact.

The defenders of Masada had an idea of what was in store for them at the hands of the Roman Flavius Silva; when their defeat seemed imminent, their leader, Eleazar, persuaded his followers to kill themselves rather than be captured and used by the Romans in their battle against Judaism. The result was 960 dead men, women, and children.

✳

ELEVEN

Tradi-Tion, Tradition, Tra-Di-Tion

A Potpourri of Jewish Traditions and Customs

Q *I know in Orthodox weddings the wedding ring goes on the index finger of the woman. Why is this?*

A In Jewish tradition, there's often a "which came first, the chicken or the egg" kind of mechanism at work.

In other words, sometimes traditions are the result of religious belief, and sometimes religious beliefs are used to explain tradition. Are you following Uncle Sol?

This may explain why two rabbis consulted about the wedding ring issue arrived at two completely different conclusions.

According to one authority, the placement of the wedding ring is connected to the theory—not a very good one, as modern science demonstrates—that the veins in the index finger provide the most direct route to the heart. This strange anatomical theory also explains why the "ring" finger has been used in Christian culture since the days of the Greeks; they just had a different notion of the so-called love vein.

Rabbi #2 came to a more Kabbalistic conclusion: wedding rings go on the index finger for numerological reasons having to do with the number 2—and a verse in the Psalms referring to God as the groom coming from the *chuppah*.

Q *Is it Jewish to worry about Friday the Thirteenth? Where does this tradition come from, anyway?*

A It's about as Jewish as a Christmas tree. Jews have a longstanding interest in numerological schemes, but somehow, we've avoided attaching any particular symbolism to this dread day.

Friday the Thirteenth legends come from the merger of two old beliefs. In the Christian world, Fridays have always had a bad reputation; Adam and Eve supposedly sinned on a Friday, and the Flood started on—you guessed it—a Friday. Christ was crucified on a Friday, and the day was thereafter the traditional day for executions.

Until recent times, it's been considered bad luck to do all kinds of things on Fridays, including starting a new job, setting sail in a ship, and turning down a bed. Financial panics have a way of starting on Fridays.

Why 13? In ancient Hindu tradition, it was considered unlucky to have 13 people at a gathering at the same time, a belief echoed in Norse mythology. The Christians took this belief and ran with it, since the Last Supper was attended by 13 guests.

Sol's religious consultants agree that the fear of Friday the Thirteenth has nothing to do with Judaism. And Friday, of course, is considered a particularly welcome day, since it represents the preparations for Shabbat.

On the other hand, if you want an unlucky day for Jews, try the ninth day of the month of Av. In a 1979 publication, the World Zionist Organization noted all manner of bad fortune coming to Jews on that date, starting with midrashic accounts of the twelve spies that Moses sent to scout out Canaan. They came back on the ninth of Av with bad news, and God told them: "On this ninth day of Av you have mourned without any cause. In future generations I will give you cause to indeed mourn on this day."

God wasn't kidding. The First and Second Temples both fell on this date; in 1492, the ninth of Av marked the decree banishing the Jews of Spain. The ninth of Av was also the date of the Chmielnicki massacres in the middle of the seventeenth century.

One might make the case that Jews have enough unlucky dates in their history to go around the calendar. But as Sol says, why take chances?

Q *How far back in Jewish history do we see the practice of getting bar mitzvahed at the age of 13? Did Jewish kids stand up in Solomon's temple and get bombarded with dictionaries and fountain pens?*

A Hardly. And think of the problems of catering . . .

First, let's clean up your language; you become bar mitzvah, you don't get bar mitzvahed.

The idea of becoming bar mitzvah as a milestone when boys assume the obligations of adult Jews goes back to Talmudic times. But the idea of the bar mitzvah celebration as we know it is of relatively recent origin. Like so many rituals in Jewish life, it has evolved considerably over the years, finally ending up in today's rubber-chicken extravaganza.

Many cultures through the aeons have assigned initiation ceremonies to the age of 13—the average age when boys hit the Big P, puberty, a word that sends shudders through the ravaged bodies of parents.

In Jewish life, the age of 13 has always been a traditional turning point for the boy—the age when the little beast begins to take on adult responsibilities, when a kid is supposed to

begin observing the commandments that define Jewish life.

But it wasn't until the fifteenth century that the bar mitzvah ceremony began to take on the qualities of a formal religious rite of passage. With increasing affluence, Western Jews invested the ceremony with increasing opulence, until we devised what novelist Herman Wouk referred to as "a blazing costly jubilee" and the "American coming-out party."

Q *Why is a silver cross considered protection against a vampire? Would a Star of David work as well? Or are vampires Jewish?*

A Although modern moviegoers generally believe that crosses do the trick, that's mostly just a bit of ethnocentricism.

Vampires, the "undead" who suck the blood of victims and proselytize the direct way—through bites on the neck—

are age-old folkloric characters in a number of different traditions.

In various cultures, vampires could be warded off with a variety of charms, amulets, and herbs, many having religious significance. The cross that works so well in the movies is just a reflection of the fact that Bram Stoker's novel about Dracula, and the never-ending stream of B-movies it spawned, are the product of a Christian-dominated culture.

As far as Sol has been able to determine, there is no close correlation to the vampire legend in Jewish tradition; thus, it would be unlikely to see Bela Lugosi cringing at the sight of, say, a menorah.

But Jewish tradition abounds with stories of supernatural creatures, including demons who crave the letters of the Hebrew alphabet in much the same way as vampires crave human blood, and *dybbuks* who may be the souls of sinners, trapped in a netherworld that is neither death nor life.

There are a variety of ways of discouraging demons in Jewish folklore, including the wearing of phylacteries and amulets and the brandishing of glowing torches.

Q *Sol, why is Chinese checkers played on a board with a Jewish star? Are we talking about a hidden community of Chinese-Jewish toy manufacturers?*

A Sorry to disappoint you, but Chinese checkers are about as Jewish—and, for that matter, as Chinese—as the Archbishop of Canterbury.

The game, which uses colored marbles and a board featuring a six-pointed star, is a modern version of a nineteenth-century English game. The updated version enjoyed a period of vogue in the United States back in the 1930s.

The hexagonal pattern of the playing board has nothing to do with Yiddishkeit. From a practical point of view, the design correlates to the playing of the game; the object, if you remember as far back as your childhood, is to move your marbles to the opposite point of the star. A six-pointed design works well for three players.

But it's also important to remember that the *Magen David* is not exclusively a Jewish symbol. The six-pointed star was a popular folkloric design in a number of cultures, including some Islamic ones. It didn't become a central symbol in Judaism until the nineteenth century.

🌟

Q *Are there Jewish faith healers?*

A To give you a precise answer, it depends. If you're talking about fellows who anoint with oil or ask the television faithful to press their afflicted flesh against the TV screen, the answer is, blessedly, no.

Judaism is a practical religion, in many ways; in the Talmud, Jews who are suffering from pain are instructed to visit a physician, not a faith healer.

But healing, of course, is part and parcel of faith and prayer; the prophets themselves were healers, when you get right down to it.

In Eastern European tradition, many rabbis developed reputations as great healers. The Ba'al Shem Tov himself, the founder of Chasidism, was known as a miracle worker, and attracted great throngs from the Eastern European Jewish world. Lesser rabbis developed similar reputations, and did a brisk business in things like amulets with curative or at least preventative powers.

The difference is that these Jewish healers did their thing only as part of their broader religious work; healing was only one element of their theological activity, not a career path in itself.

🌟

Q *Are there animals in the afterlife?*

A Sol will resist the temptation of a snide answer, like this one: "Not if we're lucky."

If you're worried that your faithful pooch might spend eternity apart from you, there's some bad news: animals, which in Jewish tradition have no permanent souls, cannot share in the afterlife. In the description of the Divine Throne, animals are mentioned—but not domestic house pets like little Rover.

Where do the pesky little critters go? They simply cease to exist. But if they have no chance for upward mobility, in the ultimate sense, at least they don't risk going in the opposite direction. Sol's own idea of gehenna is a place where everybody is required by law to have an extravagantly pruned French poodle. Imagine—an eternity spent among yapping ankle-biters. Thanks, but no thanks.

Q *How tall was Goliath? Is there any scientific evidence that a person this big really existed?*

A According to Biblical texts, Goliath was one tall dude. But how tall is another question. In First Samuel, Goliath is described as about 9 feet 9 inches tall, a real ceiling-scraper. But some Christian translations of the same texts suggest a more moderate height—about 6 feet 9 inches, about the height of your average NBA forward.

The famous scientific journal, *The Guinness Book of World Records*, tells us that the 9-foot figure may not have been beyond the realm of possibility; a fellow named Robert Pershing Wadlow was measured at 8 feet 11 inches just before his death in 1940. Wadlow was an Illinoisan, not a Philistine like Goliath.

Q *Is it Jewish to bless sneezers? This is a common custom nowadays, but I don't know if it's appropriate for an observant Jew.*

A Ah . . . CHOO. Thanks. Blessing sneezers is pretty much a universal custom; the Romans did it, American Indians did it, and Jews have done it since the days of Jacob.

Generally, authorities say the habit is based on the early belief that evil spirits can enter the body through the open mouth. Jews, anticipating modern medicine by a good bit, developed the idea that sickness could also do the same thing.

So common blessings like *gesundheit* or "health" are a kind of preventative medicine, as it were—or a statement of praise that the sneezer survived the event, since it was once believed that one could actually die from a particularly violent sneeze.

To this day, many traditional Jews use the Yiddish version of *gesundheit—zum gesund*. In Eastern Europe, some families had traditions of using a different exclamation for each of a succession of sneezes—like *zum gesund, zum leben, zum langen yahren,* and so on.

Q *My dad used to call me a "golem." Now it's nagging at me: was it a compliment, or what?*

A Sure it was a compliment, if you're flattered by being likened to a big lug with a Yiddish accent who helps smite bad guys, but usually ends up going a little haywire.

In Jewish folklore, golem are creatures fashioned out of clay and brought to life through the appropriate manipulation of holy words. The idea of the golem goes all the way back to the Psalms, but it really took off in Europe after the fifteenth century, when the idea of an avenging golem—brought to life by a *Ba'al Shem,* a "master of the Name"—gave a morale boost to Jewish communities beset by the violence of their neighbors.

Unfortunately, the golem of Jewish folklore frequently became uncontrollable, posing problems for their creators reminiscent of Boris Karloff movies. The *Frankenstein* allusion is an interesting one; the Frankenstein story, like the golem legends, emphasizes the idea of a creature created for good, but who ultimately can't control his great power.

Q *Can you recommend a rabbi who does exorcisms?*

A You think it's easy, being an Answer Man? Every week, someone wants to drag you into another religious controversy. Omniscience is not a job for the fainthearted.

But seriously: exorcism, despite its poor reputation in today's world, has been around as long as Judaism; Saul, after all, was possessed by an evil spirit that was driven out by the sounds of David's harp, a much nicer image than those provided by assorted movies about exorcism. With the rise of Kabbalism, of course, the whole matter of *dybbuks* became serious business. In the world of the *shtetl,* demons and their ilk seemed a perfectly logical explanation for the pains of everyday life. Exorcism became a well-established practice, especially during the waves of messianic fervor that occasionally swept through European Jewry.

From a modern sociological point of view, of course, there's something comforting about the idea that casting out *dybbuks* might cure afflictions like adolescence. Frankly, *dybbuks* are as good an explanation for that phenomenon as Sol has heard.

⌘

Q *I have a question about the Wall in Jerusalem. If you left a message in a crack in 1979, would it still be there today, albeit a little waterlogged? Or does someone come along and take them out periodically? What happens to old messages?*

A You have tweaked Sol's curiosity. Did you leave a message of an unseemly nature in the Wall back in your flaming youth that could embarrass you now that you are a person of some repute?

Sol posed your question to representatives of the Israeli embassy in Washington, who thought it was a pretty stupid one. Nevertheless, since they didn't have an answer either, they did some searching, and this is what they came up with.

The rabbi of the Wall, the fellow entrusted with preserving

the dignity of the site, occasionally removes messages from the cracks to avoid overcrowding.

These messages are not discarded; they are stored in jars for safekeeping, and eventually buried.

So conceivably, some future archaeologist will dig them up and wonder why, amid all the spiritually uplifting messages collected at the Wall, some boob wrote what you wrote back in 1979. This gives a whole new slant on the idea of eternity.

***

Q *Why do headstones in European Jewish cemeteries have little pebbles stacked on top? Is this some kind of mystical practice?*

A Mystical, schmystical. The pebbles are on the tombstones for the same reason that some non-Jewish cemeteries in this country have little baskets of flowers strewn about: to show that people have cared enough to visit the last resting place of the departed. It also may be related to the fact that a long time ago, before tombstones crept into Jewish practice sometime around the year 600 C.E., graves were often marked with piles of stones.

***

Q *Sol, do traditional Jewish fairy tales have wicked stepmothers? Is there a Jewish equivalent to the Cinderella story that my little girl seems to identify with so much? Snow White?*

A Do you suppose your kid's identification with Cinderella has something to do with that mop you have chained to her wrist? There are laws about that kind of thing, pal.

But let's get down to business. Sol put your question to Varda Fish, a noted expert in Jewish folklore, who kindly searched through her voluminous library in search of appropriate folk tales.

What she found was a marked lack of stepmother imagery in Jewish oral literature. Fish was able to locate only one story with a stepmother character—and, conveniently, this same tale answers your question about Cinderella.

The story is called "The Exiled Princess," and comes from somewhere in Eastern Europe. The daughter of a king is cast out of the house by her wicked stepmother. She wanders through the land, until she comes to a rabbi's house. The rabbi takes her in and turns her into a servant—not one of your more admirable characters in the annals of Jewish life.

Well, you can pretty much guess the rest. The rabbi's son falls for her, hook, line, and *tefillin*. There's a party, she dresses to the nines for the big event, and the rabbi's son gets all gooey-eyed. Instead of a glass slipper, she loses an earring; after a desperate search, the rabbi's son finds the woman with the matching earring right in his own house.

The tale ends with the usual happily-ever-after stuff. The girl and her rabbi's son go back to her real house, where she is reunited with her father. The rabbi's son becomes a prince and mazel tovs resound across the land.

In case you're thinking that Jews provided the original Cinderella, guess again: according to Fish, variants of the Cinderella legend occur in a variety of cultures. "The Exiled Princess," she said, represents a Jewish facade superimposed on a popular European tale, a common structure for such oral literature.

Alas, Fish was unable to find a Jewish equivalent of the Snow White tale. So no character will warble "Someday My Rabbi's Son Will Come" in the Disney version.

❋

Q *If the average age of puberty continues to drop for boys and girls, will Jews have to adjust the age of bar mitzvah? You know, if you hit puberty at eleven and a half, wouldn't it be only fair to become a bar mitzvah then?*

A First of all, you need to get over the notion that the changing average age for the onset of this affliction means that every boy and girl will cross that threshold at an earlier age.

So if puberty alone was the major criterion for bar mitzvah, 13 would still seem like a fairly safe bet, on average.

And let's face it, the first physical signs of puberty may have been at the root of the choice of 13 (12 for girls), but in real life, these physiological indications have never been used to actually judge whether a kid is ready to assume adult responsibilities.

In fact, the age of 13 was established in the Talmud, which means it's not likely to be changed anytime soon—no matter how much scientific data accumulates about the downward creep of puberty.

If you were serious about adjusting the age of responsibility, you might think about adjusting it *upward*. In Biblical days, children of 13 actually did begin to assume adult responsibilities; today, they're too busy listening to Mötley Crüe and figuring out new ways to torment their parents.

Q *Recently I attended an Orthodox wedding. I was expecting the traditional glass stomped by the groom; what I wasn't expecting was that the mothers of the lucky couple would break a plate before the ceremony. Why is this? Did I miss something at my own wedding?*

A Not to worry; your marriage isn't invalid because you failed to smash the crockery.

The custom came about like this. In the old days, people entered into contracts to marry off their children, sometimes when the kids were still in diapers. As one might expect, these contracts didn't always work out the way the parents intended; the result was often embarrassment and hard feelings.

Moreover, Jews, being of a legalistic bent, were uncomfortable with the idea of breaking contracts. So the custom developed of executing an oral contract for the engagement. Only just before the ceremony, when it was a cinch that the couple would get hitched, do the parents sign a formal engagement contract.

This, of course, is a cause for celebration. The ceremony takes place before the wedding. And since it is a joyous occasion, Orthodox tradition also mandates some action to remember the destruction of the Temple. It's the same as breaking the glass under the groom's foot; the idea is to inject a dose of historical memory into the joyful proceedings.

　　　　　　　　　※

Q *Sol: I recently observed some ultra-religious Jews coming from a synagogue wearing long black coats and what appeared to be fur-trimmed hats. Knowing how specific Judaism is concerning the humane treatment of animals, I was a little shocked, considering the suffering involved in trapping and killing fur-bearing animals. I would appreciate your explanation.*

A If that shocks you, take a peek at Sol's closet: all those Acryllas who gave their lives to make Sol the fashion leader that he is . . .

Different people interpret Jewish law in different ways. Some emphasize passages of Scripture showing that man was meant to make use of the animals of the world—for food, shelter, and as beasts of burden.

Early Judaism included animal sacrifices, something that would send today's animal rights advocates howling. Many Orthodox people believe animal sacrifices will be resumed after the restoration of the Temple.

But other people interested in this issue emphasize elements of Jewish law, mandating a humane approach to animals, that prohibit the infliction of needless pain.

And wearing fur for ornamentation, they suggest, constitutes a violation of the Jewish tradition, if not specific halachic pronouncements.

Rabbi Harold White, president of the International Network for Religion and Animals, notes that nothing in Jewish law mandates the wearing of fur hats, and argues that the custom contributes to the inhumane treatment of animals, not to mention the possible extinction of some species.

Obviously, some Orthodox groups do not agree. Chasidic groups began wearing these hats in the nineteenth century in Eastern Europe, in imitation of wealthy non-Jews. The fact that they were made of fur had more to do with a craving for a status symbol than religious requirements.

But once they became the fashion, they took on religious meaning. For example, there are several theories about the exact composition of these hats. One rabbi consulted by Sol indicated that this Chasidic headgear is comprised of 12 separate skins, representing the 12 Tribes of Israel; another rabbi argued that 13 was the required number, reflecting the 13 attributes of mercy.

Q *Why is blue a traditional Jewish color? You see it on prayer shawls, on all kinds of religious needlework patterns, on Chanukah wrapping paper, and the Israeli flag. I have asked several of my Jewish friends and they don't know.*

A It ain't from our baby-blue eyes.

The custom is based on the Biblical commandment to include a thread of a specific shade of blue-green in the *tsitsit*. For readers who think *tsitsit* are a species of tiny African winged insects, they are, in fact, the fringes attached to the corners of prayer shawls or the *tallis katan*—the ritual undergarment worn by your basic Orthodox Jewish man.

The specific dye was called *tekhelet;* over the centuries, there has been much debate over the sources of this particular hue.

But all controversies aside, the blue in the fringes is supposed to remind Jews of the sky, or the deep blue Mediterranean, which may remind us of God.

This symbolism became woven into the fabric of Jewish

life, to the point where Jewish kids can all identify blue as "the Jewish color," even if they don't know why.

Q *Sol, how much money would it take to make Tevya a rich man?*

A Enough to have "one long staircase just going up, one even longer going down, and more going nowhere, just for show . . ."

According to some estimates, an average *shtetl* dweller lived on an average of 150 rubles per year—at the turn of the century, about 75 dollars American.

While it is impossible to project how much Tevya's dream house might have cost, it's clear that the cheerful dairyman would have *felt* rich with a few thousand rubles in his pocket.

TWELVE

Adventures and Mis-Adventures in Jewish Eating

Q *Sol, my grandmother used to complain that the gefilte fish we eat in this country is nothing like the* real stuff *they used to get in the Old Country. What's the difference?*

A Gefilte fish has gotten something of a bad rap in recent years, mostly because of the fact that many of the bottled variants of the delicacy, available on your supermarket shelves, taste sort of like marshmallows soaked in a pan along with old gym socks.

What your grandmother was probably referring to is the fact that what we take to be gefilte fish here in this country is closer to what our European cousins once called *"falsche fish"*—imitation fish.

In European lands with access to fresh fish, gefilte fish was originally a fish stuffing; they'd take carp, white fish, or some other fine finned specimen, grind it up, add onions, matzah meal, and eggs, and stuff the whole mess back inside the fish skin.

In countries like Hungary, where fish were harder to come by, they invented *falsche* fish. It was white-meat chicken, chopped up finely, mixed with eggs and all the rest—and served in loaves or balls with a jellied sauce, much like today's gefilte fish, American style.

Q *Solly, what is the meaning of the different kinds of lox? Why is Nova lox salty and belly lox isn't? Don't say anything to disgust me.*

A Worry not; your delicate gut is safe in Uncle Sol's tender hands.

Nova lox, short for lox from Nova Scotia salmon, is not salty for a very good reason; it's a freshwater salmon that is used to make the stuff.

In contrast, belly lox is derived from a saltwater variety of the fish.

But the meaning of "belly" in belly lox is somewhat unclear. Sol's favorite deli owner, Jerry Terlitzky, suggests that it has something to do with the part of the saltwater fish used for lox, but he sensibly urged Sol not to risk his worldwide reputation as a Know It All on that answer.

So Sol is issuing a call to lox historians everywhere: does anybody out there know why belly lox is called belly lox? Sol will print the least ridiculous answer in an upcoming edition.

Note to Readers:

In a recent column, Sol expressed bafflement about why we call the salty variety of lox "belly lox." Sure enough, some loud-mouthed readers responded with varying degrees of expertise. The most authoritative-sounding answer came from Seymour Attman, the bagel baron of Lombard Street in

Baltimore. His answer, condensed somewhat, follows. Thanks, Sy, and Sol will ignore your concluding attempt at humor.

Dear Sol:

I read your comments of January 6, and would like to be of help about belly lox.

The salmon, when they are caught, are cut in half lengthwise and cured in brine in hogshead barrels. After a period of curing, the salmon are smoked. After this, the belly of the salmon is cut out, starting from near the head, to where the belly tapers off. This part of the lox is fatter in quality and texture. It's like the difference between wool and cashmere in texture. Calorie-wise, the regular lox and belly lox are the same. But the texture of the belly makes it more of a quality product.

P.S. These answers are not ridiculous but true.

P.P.S. I leave you with a joke. How come you can't keep Jews in jail? Because they eat lox!

Q *Where does the word "bialy" come from? Why don't people outside New York understand the difference between a bialy and a bagel?*

A The second part of your question ranks right up there with "Who put the ram in the ramalama ding-dong." At Sol's local bagel emporium they have no problem telling bagels and bialys apart; they charge twice as much for a bialy. We may be ignoramuses, but the free market knows the truth.

But let's get serious: while "bagel" is a descriptive term, derived from the Yiddish word for "ring," "bialy" is geographical—coming from Bialystok, the Polish village known for its hungry Jewish population. There is also speculation that "bialy" comes from the Russian word for "white," as in Byelo (White) Russia.

Many Jews have the mistaken notion that bagels are an American invention. Not true; in fact, Leo Rosten, the dean of Yiddish language and lore, cites a Polish regulation dating from 1610, which promised bagels for women giving birth.

But the fortuitous combination of bagels and lox did originate on these shores.

Q *What is lutefisk? My local grocery started carrying it, and it looks like it might be worth trying. Is it* treife?

A To say that lutefisk is worth trying is like saying that industrial waste might make a good hors d'oeuvre. Sol is all for being open-minded, but there's such a thing as going too far.

Lutefisk is a substance consumed by some residents of the Upper Midwest. What it is, basically, is old codfish, soaked in enough lime to start a quarry. Folks out there prove their mettle by eating the stuff and surviving.

In Scandinavian-American culture, lutefisk serves much the same purpose as *shchav* does among Jews. In other words, it's a point of ethnic pride that they voluntarily eat something that the rest of the world thinks is more suited to industrial applications.

Is it *treife?* If Sol remembers his dietary laws correctly, acceptable fish must have both fins and scales, which means that cod is okay. But the regulations don't mention anything about odor and taste; open a package of lutefisk, and it'll peel the paint from your walls and polish your silver all at the same time. So you're on your own, bubbe. Eat it at your own risk.

Q *Recently, I talked to somebody who is convinced that tomatoes and cheese on a matzah was the first pizza. Is this true? Please advise.*

A Please understand that every ethnic group in our plural-istic society likes to decline responsibility for its nastier forms

of ethnic food—and claim credit for the tastier delicacies of other groups.

So no self-respecting Jew will admit to any cultural affinity for, say, *derma,* a food reportedly on the EPA's latest list of toxic chemicals.

But Jews love to take credit for things like chop suey and pizza, despite not a shred of evidence to support these claims. And Sol once encountered a man of Chinese extraction who insisted that his forebears had invented the bagel.

Pizza, for your information, is generally regarded to be of Neapolitan origin. One of the early definitions of the product is that it is made with a "yeast dough," thus precluding matzah as the prototype.

Pizza was imported to this country in the early part of this century; the first pizza joint appeared in New York in 1905. This country's contribution to pizza included toppings like sausage, anchovies, and other highly suspect substances.

Q *What precautions should a Jewish garbageman take when carrying away the waste of a gentile family that eats pork?*

A *Kashrut* is one thing, paranoia is something else again. The dietary laws say you can't *eat* pork; they don't say anything about proximity to this particular substance.

Interestingly, most authorities suggest that from a strictly technical point of view, pork is no more objectionable than other non-kosher animals, like zebras, wolves, and hippopotamuses.

Old Jewish folklore suggests that one reason for the particularly strong aversion towards pigs is the fact that they are "deceptive" animals.

That is, pigs have one of the requirements of approved animals—split hooves. But they lack the ability to chew their cuds, the other requirement. When pigs sleep, they are one of few animals to do so with their rear legs sticking out—as if to say, so the legend goes, "Look at me, I'm kosher, you can see my hooves."

Whether or not pigs are clever liars, pork came to symbolize the entire issue of *kashrut*, since it was among the few *treife* animals popular in the diets of the societies in which Jews found themselves. Let's face it: fillet of bat was never the issue here.

But there is also a strong cultural aversion that goes far beyond the technical details of *kashrut*. The image of the pig is part and parcel of Jewish history, starting with Antiochus Epiphanes' attempts to force Jews to sacrifice pigs in the Temple. Pig imagery was often used to taunt Jews in the Middle Ages, as well.

The aversion to pigs has become tightly woven into Jewish culture, so much so that even many people who wouldn't know how to run a kosher kitchen if you held knives to their throats feel a powerful revulsion toward the poor pig.

As for your Jewish garbageman—this is not exactly a big fraternity, but there are a few out there—he isn't in halachic jeopardy, unless he has very bizarre and unhealthy dietary habits.

Q *Mom says corned beef and pastrami are the same cut of meat, just prepared differently; I say phooey. What about you?*

A Not only are you inarticulate, bubbe, you're wrong; *never* question a Jewish mom about food.

Corned beef and pastrami are both cut from the brisket of the cow. Actually, the pastrami is cut from the top part of the brisket, while the corned beef generally involves the whole shmeer.

The difference is in the preparation. Corned beef is—you

guessed it—corned, which is basically the same as pickled. Pastrami, on the other hand, is seasoned with peppercorns and other goodies and baked.

Next time, better you should listen to your mom when it comes to food.

※

Q *Sol, a bunch of us were sitting around talking about nasty-tasting ethnic foods. Some of my Jewish friends gave the nod to borscht as the most revolting food in the Jewish repertoire. Now I happen to like borscht. I maintain* shchav *is the ultimate Jewish culinary nightmare. Can you mediate this dispute?*

A If you like borscht, you probably also like old radiator water, bubbe. But you are right on one count: *shchav,* which is basically sour grass soup, is one reason Jewish cuisine has an unfortunate reputation for toxicity, despite a number of truly superb dishes.

Recently, Sol put the question of hideous Jewish foods to Avi West, associate director of the Board of Jewish Education of Greater Washington.

West, who is second to none in his appreciation of things Jewish, did not mince words. "I haven't seen anything the color of *shchav* since my elementary school walls," West said. "It's the closest thing in the Jewish world to acid rain."

Shchav is roughly equivalent to what the French call "sorrel soup," only made with more pungent and possibly corrosive ingredients.

West also weighed in with his opinion that genuine Russian borscht, made with meat as well as beets, is even more toxic than the Jewish variety, describing the smell of this substance in terms too graphic for a family magazine.

And Sol might add a food still enjoyed by some older members of our community, for reasons beyond any hope of comprehension: jellied calves feet, or *ptcha.* One expert in Jewish food preparation described the preparation of this delicacy: after boiling the nasty-looking mess for many hours, take the part that looks somewhat edible and throw it away. What's left is what you choke down—if you have the wherewithal.

Sol will pass on this one, thank you.

※

Q *Why are clams and lobster and really yummy seafood considered* treife? *Sol, give me a good scientific explanation other than "See Leviticus 32:3."*

A Sol is all for modern science, but in this case, science comes up with some pretty farfetched guesses about the origins of *kashrut*.

Shellfish are included in the category of "swarming things of the water and all other living creatures that are in the water," according to Leviticus 11:10. This includes clams, frogs, lobsters, oysters, scallops, shrimps, and—just in case you have weird tastes—jellyfish and sponges.

It does not apply to sponge cake, a food often considered to be the closest thing to indigenous Jewish cuisine.

For the Orthodox, this is explanation enough, and they do not take kindly to "scientific" explanations for the origins of the dietary laws.

For others, there has been no end of speculation about the origins of these prohibitions. There have been theories that shellfish are particularly hospitable to various micro-organisms, and that that's the "reason" for the prohibition, or that ancient man somehow instinctively understood that these critters were scavengers, and therefore not fit to be eaten.

But if the human race is so darned smart, why did we invent, say, Cheez Doodles, or "call waiting"? Leviticus sounds at least as plausible as a bunch of Neanderthal Mr. Wizards, studying the culinary habits of crabs and concluding scientifically that they were not fit as dinner. Implausibility is purely in the eyes of the beholder.

※

Q *Dear Sol: Is there any real significance to the fact that both doughnuts and bagels have holes in the center? It seems mighty strange to me.*

A Is this supposed to be a trick question? Are you trying to get Sol to say something about "one-world" conspiracies and the Masons?

Forget it: when Sol sniffs out conspiracies, he'll find his own, thank you.

Doughnuts and bagels are similar in shape for a very mundane reason. When dealing with heavy lumps of dough, it's never easy to cook them just right, so that the centers do not taste like molten moon rock.

The hole in the doughnut or bagel allows the cooking medium—oil, in the case of doughnuts, water in the case of bagels—to be more evenly applied to every part of the product, thus eliminating those indigestible centers.

This is not just idle speculation; Sol put the theory to the test in his own kitchen, which is admittedly not a place that would send Julia Child into paroxysms of envy.

The results were dramatic. Two bagels of identical thickness were boiled for the same amount of time, one a traditional bagel, the other a mutant without a hole.

The bagel with the hole was succulent and perfectly cooked. The non-holed bagel was fine on the outside, hideously undercooked in the center. In the interests of science, Sol then fed this latter sample to a neighborhood dog, who has not been seen since.